C000091503

CURIOUS
AND SURPRISING
VICTORIAN
DERBYSHIRE

GLYN JONES

HALSGROVE

First published in Great Britain in 2015

Copyright © Glyn Jones 2015
Newspaper extracts © The British Library Board. All rights reserved.
Included with permission of The British Newspaper Archive

British Library Cataloguing-in-Publication Data
A CIP record for this title is available from the British Library

ISBN 978 0 85704 264 4

HALSGROVE
Halsgrove House,
Ryelands Business Park,
Bagley Road, Wellington, Somerset TA21 9PZ
Tel: 01823 653777   Fax: 01823 216796
email: sales@halsgrove.com

Part of the Halsgrove group of companies
Information on all Halsgrove titles is available at: www.halsgrove.com

Printed in China by the Everbest Printing Co Ltd

Contents

A typical Victorian Derbyshire street with its inn.

CHAPTER ONE

Feud, Flight and Scandal

Today, a visitor to Alfreton Hall would find just one remaining wing of a country house standing prominently in its extensive grounds. In 1881 its much grander predecessor was the scene of an event that would shock local people, attract worldwide interest and see its participants embroiled in a society scandal.

Alfreton Hall was the home of the Palmer-Morewood family. It was described in the *New York Times* of 1882 as "a pleasant mansion situated on one of the uplands overlooking the Erewash Valley, just where the green plains of Nottinghamshire rise into the wooded heights of the Peak of Derbyshire."

Alfreton Hall – the former home of the Palmer-Morewoods.

Alfreton Hall in the early years of the nineteenth century.

The Palmer-Morewoods were a successful county family. By the last quarter of the nineteenth-century they had made a great deal of money from their land and mining interests.

However, in December 1881, the Palmer-Morewood family were not experiencing a sense of harmony. Charles Rowland Palmer-Morewood J.P., who resided at Alfreton Hall, was involved in a protracted dispute with his four younger brothers. It involved the payment of money from the will of their late father.

In 1873, Charles Palmer-Morewood the elder, had left sums of money to his five sons, his four daughters and his wife. Charles Palmer-Morewood the younger, as the eldest son, had also taken control of a colliery and plant valued at £27,000. By 1881, his four younger brothers were claiming that they had not received their full entitlement and were demanding £63,000 as a settlement.

On Christmas morning 1881, George, Alfred, Ernest and William Palmer-Morewood set off to spend Christmas at Alfreton Hall with their elder brother and their mother. They called first at South Wingfield where they had some lunch and wine at the Vicarage with the Rev. F.W. Christian.

The brothers then moved on to the residence of Mr J. B. Wilson where they drank more wine. Here, they persuaded Wilson's teenage son to join them as they made their way to the Hall.

At first, events at Alfreton Hall were very festive and traditional. Contemporary accounts describe "a Yule Log burning brightly" and "holly bough hung over family portraits". A good evening was had by all.

At 10 p.m. the five brothers gathered to say goodnight to their mother. Mrs Palmer-Morewood made the short journey to her son George's house at Hallfield Gate where she was staying.

The gentlemen then withdrew to the Smoking Room. Here the quality of a valuable old rum was discussed as it was quickly despatched. Then, suddenly, and without any warning, Charles Palmer-Morewood was grabbed and dragged into the Library.

The door was locked from the inside and Charles was asked to sign a document giving his brothers the sum of money they were still contesting from their father's will. Charles refused – and continued to do so even when threatened with violence.

Some dramatic accounts tell of the brothers having drawn lots to decide who would kill Charles if that became necessary. This may have either been bravado on the part of the brothers or invention on the part of the fascinated Derbyshire public.

There is also talk of a revolver being pressed against his head. The weapon was supposed to have been "in the passage" at Alfreton Hall although it was never seen or found.

A violent struggle certainly occured. Charles, at one point, managed to grab a bell-pull to summon his butler for help. When the butler dutifully arrived, William went alone to the door and, as a pretence, sent him off for some water whilst Charles was held at bay.

The brothers continued to assault Charles but, amazingly, he managed to grab the bell-pull a second time. This time the butler was informed that the brothers were just indulging in "a little jollity".

At around 1 a.m. the younger Palmer-Morewoods left Alfreton Hall to go home allegedly remarking to the butler "go to the Library, you will find your Master lying very drunk".

The Squire was discovered lying in a pool of his own blood. He was virtually naked – he was wearing just one stocking and there was a tattered piece of cloth around his neck.

It appeared from injuries to his nose and cheeks that he had been dragged about the floor. He was covered in bruises and had wounds to his

Hallfield Gate – the home of George Palmer-Morewood.

leg and the back of his head. Doctor Bingham from Alfreton was sent for immediately as was Doctor Dolman, a surgeon, from Derby.

Blissfully, Charles's wife was ill at the time and so she did not witness events that would have done little to aid her recovery. Equally, young Mr Wilson who had accompanied the brothers to the Hall was spared – he had remained in the Smoking Room !

The news of events at Alfreton Hall caused shock and interest in equal levels. A warrant for the arrest of George, Alfred, Ernest and William Palmer-Morewood was issued.

On Tuesday 27 December 1881 the four young men were apprehended at Clay Cross – George's house at Hallfield Gate was nearby. Alfred, Ernest and William all resided at Wigwell Grange which was a little further away near Wirksworth.

The brothers were taken to the "lock-up" in Alfreton, where they spent the night prior to being taken to the Magistrates' Office in High Street. Here they were given bail, each brother bound over with £500 of their own money and a further £500 stood by their "bondsmen".

Mr Parkin, a pawnbroker from Alfreton stood surety for George Palmer-Morewood.

Alfred was supported by Mr Harris a solicitor from Crich. A surgeon from Alfreton, Mr Fielding pledged support for Ernest. The Reverend Christian from South Wingfield came forward for William.

No evidence was taken at the Magistrates' Office. The case was scheduled to be heard on the following Monday morning at 11.30 a.m.

The defendants were charged with the offence of "common assault". This caused a good deal of debate locally with most people expecting more serious charges. However, the lesser charge was in keeping with the family's wish to play down events. The whole episode was referred to as a "nine days' wonder" in some quarters but this dismissive stance did not reflect public opinion in general. There was a deep sense of shock and outrage.

Charles Palmer-Morewood had only just recovered sufficiently to attend. He was, understandably, angry, but preferred that his assailants be "bound over to keep the peace" rather than suffer severe punishment.

Monday morning's hearing duly arrived. The four Palmer-Morewood brothers failed to attend. Apparently, they had received "judicious counsel" to adopt this tactic to avoid being speedily processed by the imminent January Quarter Sessions.

It was not the first time some of these young men had shown an apparent disregard for the law. Two years previously Ernest and Alfred had been due to appear before Magistrates in Belper accused of being "drunk and disorderly in a public thoroughfare". Their non-appearance prompted a rather critical editorial in the local press – "it is regretted that these young sparks have not yet learned what a summons means."

Charles Palmer-Morewood tried to clarify some things at the Alfreton hearing even though his brothers were absent. He was at pains to point out that stories of drunken excess at Alfreton Hall on Christmas Day were exaggerated. He outlined the alcohol consumption in great detail – a half bottle of sherry, one bottle of light claret, two bottles of champagne, another pint bottle of light claret and a bottle of rum. The latter, he helpfully, explained, contained ten "ordinary wine glass measures".

Charles emphasised that, at no point, did he see a revolver.

Nobody present seemed to know the whereabouts of the brothers. Mr Barker, who was advising Mr Harris, one of the "bondsmen", also represented the defendants. He said " I am informed that the defendants have not been seen in town this morning. Indeed, from information that has reached me today I shall not be surprised if they do not appear."

There was much speculation surrounding where they had gone. They had last been seen together at Wigwell Grange. The lane from Wigwell led to "several excellent turnpikes leading to Buxton, Derby and other large towns." The Palmer-Morewoods would then have able to travel by rail wherever they pleased.

A warrant was issued for their arrest. There was some discussion about amending the charges to more serious ones but this was deemed inappropriate.

By early January it was widely believed that the four brothers had made their way south, initially to London

The lack of definite sightings of the Palmer-Morewood fugitives only served to feed a frenzy of speculation.

It is at this point that another intriguing aspect of these events emerges. Ellen Miller-Mundy, a society beauty from Shipley Hall in Derbyshire had recently left her husband and taken up with the young Charles Henry John Chetwynd-Talbot, the twentieth Earl of Shrewsbury. Ellen was the sister of the Palmer-Morewood brothers.

Indeed, Captain Mundy, Ellen's husband, had enlisted the help of her family when she first went to the Continent with the Earl. There was a dramatic pursuit first to Paris and then to Strasbourg. Eventually, in frantic and chaotic circumstances all parties found themselves on the same train!

Ellen was brought back to England where it was hoped some reconciliation could take place. This proved a forlorn hope. In December 1881 Ellen and Captain Mundy were divorced, paving the way for her marriage to Shrewsbury in June 1882.

In early January 1882 the Earl of Shrewsbury and Ellen set sail from Eastbourne on board his yacht the *Castalia*. They intended to be in the Mediterranean until March.

The timing of this departure fuelled the theory that the four fugitives had been spirited away by their sister. The *New York Times* felt confident

The House of Confinement – Alfreton's lock-up. The Palmer- Morewoods were kept here overnight.

enough in the edition dated 29 January 1882 to repeat a story that had reached their correspondent's ears from Derbyshire:

"One account reaches us from Alfreton declares they (the Palmer-Morewoods) are about to embark on a cruise in the Mediterranean in the beautiful yacht of the Earl of Shrewsbury."

It went on –

"These four young aesthetes, their divorced and divine sister and the lordly libertine" says my correspondent "will make, no doubt, a merry crew."

The Earl of Shrewsbury was furious when he read about these stories in a number of publications. On 4 February 1882 the *Derbyshire Times and Chesterfield Herald* published letter from the Earl to the Editor of the Daily News :

"Sir, I have just seen the *Daily News* of the 23rd inst. In which I see under the heading of 'Nice':

'There are several yachts in the harbour both at Nice and Villafranche, including Lord Shrewsbury's *Castalia*, on board which are the brothers Morewood who recently left England.'

As there is not the slightest foundation in the report (which has been largely spread about) that the brothers Morewood are on the *Castalia*, I shall be obliged if you will contradict the statement in your next edition.

Shrewsbury, Yacht *Castalia*, Monaco January 27th."

The level of indignation felt by the Earl of Shrewsbury appeared to be justified as the brothers were, apparently, in America. In March 1882 the *Manchester Evening News* reported that George Palmer-Morewood had authorised the sale of his farming stock at Hallfield Gate. Moreover, his housekeeper had set sail with George's dog and his silver.

The American sojourn did not begin well. In August William Palmer – Morewood was to die in Charlottesville Virginia from an attack of typhoid fever. His funeral was not only attended by most of the local leading citizens, but also by a large number of "his countrymen" settled in the State. William had clearly made an impression during his brief time in Charlottesville as banks and shops were closed as a mark of respect.

The funeral procession included two of William's brothers – George and Alfred. Interestingly, a Mr George Siddall from Alfreton was also recorded as being in attendance. The mourners in Virginia were under the impression that William's remains would be repatriated and placed in the family vault in Alfreton.

William's American estate was reported to be in excess of £12,000 in value. Alfred and Ernest Augustus were each left £5,000 in the will.

The surviving brothers seemed intent on remaining in the United States. In November 1882 Hallfield Gate held a sale of "superior household furniture". Entire dining room, drawing room and breakfast room features in mahogany, oak and walnut were sold. Bedroom suites in polished pine also went under the hammer.

The lavishly furnished Billiard Room was sacrificed in a lot described as having "an excellent table by 'Burroughs and Watts' with pyramid, pool and billiard cues etc." Included was a six light chandelier with shades.

The events at Alfreton Hall on Christmas Day 1881 continued to have a deep impact on the lives of those involved. It is ironic that the United States should prove such a welcoming haven for the Palmer-Morewood brothers. The *New York Times* had gone further than simply reporting events January 1882. Its article was keen to point out that the "civilised savages" were reported to be "laughing at the law in France or Spain". It concluded by questioning whether those lower down the social scale may have enjoyed quite as much liberty.

CHAPTER TWO

An Unexpected French Connection

Students and shoppers scurry past the gravestone situated in a small section of St Mary's churchyard in Chesterfield. It is partly carved in French and commemorates the death, in March 1812, of Francois Raingeard aged thirty years. The memorial provides a link to a most remarkable story.

At the beginning of the nineteenth century England was involved in a war with Napoleon's France. French prisoners of war were held in England and the wealthier officers were given the opportunity to avoid the squalid conditions of the prison hulk ships. Fifty towns in England were designated "parole towns" – Chesterfield was amongst them.

In 1803 a large number of high ranking naval and army officers arrived in Chesterfield. They accepted the terms of their parole which included a restriction on travel beyond one mile from the town centre. They received an allowance of half a guinea a week.

A number of them had recently seen action in Haiti and had been involved in the suppression of the slave rebellion. Toussaint L'Ouverture, the talented leader of the rebels, was heavily influenced by French writers. He welcomed the ideas that had fuelled the French Revolution. Toussaint L'Ouverture was badly treated by Napoleon and died in captivity. Many of the French officers were uncomfortable with events in Haiti.

Consequently, they were not always united as a group. General Rochambeau and General Boyer were removed from Chesterfield because their fellow officers disapproved of their over-zealous treatment of the supporters of Toussaint L'Ouverture. The tense atmosphere threatened the peace of their settlement in North Derbyshire.

The situation caused by the presence of Rochambeau and Boyer was not the only example of discord amongst the French. Colonel Richemont had a large sum of money stolen from a strongbox in his lodgings at "The Falcon" public house. The culprit proved to be a fellow officer who was so embarrassed by events he took poison, and when this proved inadequate,

A poignant reminder of some   *Wingerworth Hall.*
Napoleonic guests.

stabbed himself to death.

The "one-mile" restriction on travel was destined to provide the whole Chesterfield contingent with a practical difficulty. Sir Thomas Windsor Hunloke of Wingerworth Hall was a Roman Catholic and had a Catholic chapel on his estate. Unfortunately, the chapel was more than a mile away from the town centre.

Sir Thomas sympathised with the plight of the French officers and was keen to offer them hospitality, and the opportunity to worship, at Wingerworth. He mobilised estate staff to move the milestone " just a little down the road, past our gate". The chapel was no longer out of bounds !

Visiting Wingerworth Hall proved to be an adventure as well as a convenience for the French. Sir Thomas had begun assembling a collection of animals for his menagerie. One of the officers was startled when he encountered an escaped bear in the grounds. This was a genuine hazard as the menagerie was home to two American brown bears, a Russian bear – not to mention wolves, dogs and exotic birds.

Sir Thomas, ironically to die in Paris in 1817, was not the only member of the Hunloke family to socialise with the French. James Hunloke, his brother, entertained the French prisoners at Birdholme House. At one meal James was forced to describe a haunch of venison as fish in the company of the French to spare any awkwardness linked to diet and faith. The guests readily joined in the joke and, on subsequent visits, any forbidden food was always blamed on the cook.

Many French officers were linked with Freemasonry and Chesterfield's group was no exception. Under a French rule seven "master masons" could form a lodge.

In fact, two lodges were formed in the town between 1809 and 1812 – the "Loge de L'Esperance" (hope) and the "Loge de St Jerome et L'Esperance". Such names were common across the country and reflected their feelings and circumstances.

The Scarsdale Lodge was also visited by the French on at least eight occasions and, certainly, attended on 5 March 1810 when "Hy Vinclair and R. de la Croix, two foreigners, visited this night."

The French contributed to the local economy during their stay. A specialised small scale glove making industry developed. The gloves were netted and pegged with a single needle. Demand for this neat and desirable product spread amongst fashion conscious ladies. Sadly, the departure of the officers seemed to coincide with the demise of the product.

Across the country 462 officers broke their parole and escaped to France – although no freemasons were amongst them !

Chesterfield had two high-profile fugitives. General Excelmans and Colonel de la Grange successfully escaped to France in a covered cart aided by a local man, James Lowton. The latter ended up in Derby gaol for his trouble.

The unfortunate General D'Henin was not the only French officer to have links with the local community. A Polish servant to Col. Philip de Gaetze stayed behind and became a farmer.

When the French were allowed to return home in 1814 many in Chesterfield were genuinely sad. They had been a positive presence in the town. Many were excellent craftsmen and carved intricate models from bone and ivory.

General Excelmans was to join up with Napoleon on his return from exile and experienced defeat on the battlefield at Waterloo in 1815. He was in good company. General Charles D'Henin had married a lady of Scottish background whilst in Chesterfield and he, too, had rejoined Napoleon. General D'Henin lost a leg in the battle.

The officers had become a regular sight walking through the town, following their route along High Street and Middle Pavement. It was observed, as late as 1903, that "these gentlemen with their patois and grace of deportment, gave piquancy to the life of the town."

In Chesterfield we still have a memory of Francois Raingeard "Prisonnier de Guerre" who, two hundred years ago, died "in Friendship" on 10 March 1812.

CHAPTER THREE

A Man Scorned

Wigwell Grange is an attractive Grade II listed country mansion. In the nineteenth century it was adjacent to a quiet turnpike road. In 1863 this picturesque rural location was to be the scene of a brutal murder.

The events at Wigwell Grange were followed and keenly debated way beyond the boundaries of Derbyshire. Sir George Grey, the Home Secretary no less, was called upon for legal guidance.

The beginning of the story is far from unusual. Elizabeth Caroline Goodwin, aged twenty-two, had exchanged letters with her fiancé, George Victor Townley who was a few years older. These communications had proved to be upsetting for George Townley. Elizabeth, or Bessie as she was known locally, had decided to call off their engagement in a letter on 14 August 1863.

The pair had met whilst Bessie had been staying with relatives in Manchester and they had just become engaged in the summer of 1863. Townley was an affluent young gentleman whose family owned a successful business.

However, Bessie had recently taken up with another man – something she neglected to disclose to Townley. Instead, Bessie blamed her reluctance to commit to Townley on the opposition of key members of her family. She cited the fact that he appeared to have no independent means.

Townley was keen to try and resolve things between himself and Bessie. On Friday 21 August he arrived at Whatstandwell Station and quickly made his way to the "Bulls Head".

Ann Bailey, the landlady, recalled Townley arriving at 11.00 a.m. He immediately enquired if there was a note that had been left for him. He was told that there was nothing. Townley asked for a bed for the night and he left his carpet bag before indulging in a glass of brandy and water. He took a pill with a second glass of brandy before purchasing some cold water on his departure.

Townley made his way to see the Rev. Herbert Harris who kept the Grammar School in Wirksworth. Here he told Harris about the engagement, the exchange of letters and the current situation. Harris confirmed to Townley that it was his understanding that the engagement was, indeed, off.

Townley pressed Harris about the rumours about a "fellow clergyman" who had been spending a great deal of time at Wigwell Grange visiting Bessie and her grandfather. Harris was careful not too reveal too much detail to Townley even though he suspected that there "was an engagement between this clergyman and Miss Goodwin."

It was clear that Townley wanted to see Bessie and hear it from her own lips that their engagement was truly over. Rev. Harris believed that Townley was behaving perfectly normally given the circumstances.

Harris advised Townley to write a note to Bessie requesting a meeting but Townley was a quite downcast at this suggestion – he had already tried that tactic. Harris said Townley might try calling at Wigwell Grange and enquiring if Bessie would see him. Townley seemed to accept that this was the preferred course of action saying that "I will do so and get it off my mind."

As the time moved on to 2 p.m. Harris excused himself as he had to go to fulfil duties in the school. He did, though, offer to meet with Townley later on after he had called at Wigwell Grange. Their second meeting would not take place.

On leaving Rev. Harris, Townley made his way to Wigwell Grange. He knocked on the door and was admitted by the housemaid, Margaret Poyser. Bessie was found and, reluctantly, agreed to meet with her former fiancé.

Townley and Bessie went to the library but soon left the house to walk in the grounds. Once outside, they sat for half an hour on a garden seat and were observed deep in conversation. At one point, Bessie returned to the house but soon returned.

At 7.15 p.m the couple were seen on the neighbouring turnpike road by a local miller, Thomas Biddulph. They were talking and Biddulph recalls overhearing the words "quarter past nine" as he passed. He believed that they were discussing the time of a train.

Shortly afterwards Reuben Conway, a labourer, walked along the turnpike road. He was alerted by a "moaning sound". He ran forward and encountered Bessie Goodwin. She was clinging to the wall by the side of the road.

Bessie's face was covered in blood and there was more blood down the front of her dress. Bessie asked Conway to help her back to Wigwell Grange – she also told him that there was a man just down the road who "had been murdering her".

Conway put his arm around Bessie to try to help her to stand. She was still anxious, despite her serious wounds, and asked if Conway could see anyone behind them. At this point, Conway spotted a man about 60 yards away.

George Townley crossed the road and went up to Conway. The latter confronted the stranger and asked "who has been murdering Miss Goodwin ?" Townley admitted that he had stabbed the young woman.

Conway asked Townley to help him carry Bessie back to the Grange. Townley took hold of her head, Conway her body.

Conway was surprised by Townley's behaviour towards his victim. He remembers him using the word "poor" several times as he addressed Bessie. He also ominously said "you should not have proved false to me".

They were struggling to carry Bessie and staunch the flow of blood. Conway laid Bessie down and asked if Townley would continue to assist whilst he ran for more help.

Conway went to Mr Bowmer's yard where he worked and returned in a matter of minutes. Townley was on the ground next to Bessie holding some cloth tightly against her neck. Conway asked if she was still alive, Townley said she was. At this point, Bessie murmured "take me home".

One of the men who had hurried to help Conway asked Townley who had stabbed Miss Goodwin, Townley replied "I have done it".

Bessie did not quite make it home. Shortly after she was picked up again Townley noticed that she was dead. She was placed on the ground, Townley knelt down and kissed her.

Captain Goodwin, Bessie's grandfather, had come to the gate of Wigwell Grange with Mrs Poyser. It was at this point that the elderly gentleman was told of the death of his granddaughter.

The eighty-year-old Captain Goodwin reacted in a very strange fashion. He calmly enquired if anyone knew who was responsible for the murder of Bessie. Townley told Captain Goodwin that he was the killer. Captain Goodwin took Townley by the arm and led him into the house, asking why he had done it. Townley replied "she has deceived me, and the woman who has deceived me, she must die."

The grandfather and the murderer sat drinking tea in the library of Wigwell Grange. Townley was clear about his fate … "I shall be hanged", he said. He was also keen to point out that Bessie "knew my temper". Townley asked Captain Goodwin to look after his watch and his money. Captain Goodwin refused to do this.

Next, Townley produced two packets of letters exchanged between himself and Bessie. He told Captain Goodwin that he did not want the contents read out in open court. He asked Goodwin to burn them after he had read them.

P.C. Parnell had a very straightforward task on arriving at Wigwell Grange later on the evening. Townley gave himself up for the murder of Bessie and said he would "go quietly" if he were allowed to see his victim once more.

Parnell asked Townley if he still had the murder weapon. A pocket knife was produced from his pocket – it was closed but still wet with blood. He was then escorted to the "lock-up" in nearby Wirksworth. Little was said on the short journey but as they neared their destination Townley announced – "I am far more happy than I was before; and trust she is."

The trial of George Victor Townley in December 1863 aroused great interest. The case was unique in Derbyshire because the perpetrator and victim were both gentry. Consequently a ticketing system was utilised to control the large numbers wishing to attend the proceedings in Derby. The demand was such that the Court could have been filled "twenty or thirty times over".

Townley had acquitted himself well since his incarceration in Derby Gaol. He had been quiet and reserved. He was subject to all normal rules and regulations but had been permitted to have his "victuals" supplied to him from the County Hotel.

The County Hotel accommodated members of the Townley family during the trial. The parents of the accused were supported by Townley's sister and other close relatives. Captain Goodwin and the Wigwell Grange party had taken rooms at the Midland Hotel.

On the first day of the trial there were forty-five police officers on duty. The police inspected tickets at every turn. The Court was full to capacity with not only ticket holders but also anyone who could claim to have business in the building. A glimpse of George Victor Townley was eagerly sought and anticipated.

The galleries and the main body of the Court were filled with the cream of Derby society. A great many ladies were present. The "lower orders" were ticketless and outside. They had to content themselves with peeping through the railings.

The Derwent Whatstandwell, formerly the Bulls Head.

Coat of arms – detail in the wall bordering Wigwell Grange. Bessie Goodwin was carried past here.

The prisoner arrived in the dock. He was wearing a black suit and seemed unmoved by the throng that greeted him. He looked more pale and haggard than he had when he was first arrested.

The barristers were already present – Mr Boden Q.C. for the prosecution, Messrs Macauley, O'Brien and Fitzjames Stephen for the defence. There was a large contingent of the press with all the major London and principal journals represented.

The trial began at 10.00 a.m.. Townley was asked to enter a plea. " Not guilty" he replied in firm tone. The anticipated plea of insanity had, seemingly, been abandoned by the defence.

Townley bent his head and looked downwards as the jurors' names were called. An observer noted that "his countenance has nothing in it that would indicate him as a person capable of committing the atrocious crime with which he stands charged."

The facts of the case were briefly stated by the prosecution. Dr Newton Mant from Wirksworth was called. He had examined the body of Bessie Goodwin on 21 August. He recalled three wounds to the right side of her neck. There was a stab wound behind and below the right ear. There was a second, more superficial, stab wound and a third wound, further in front. This third wound was 3 inches long and extended nearly to the chin.

A large clasp knife was then produced in Court and identified as the weapon.

Mr Macauley questioned Townley at length for the defence. Crucially, for later developments, he was trying to establish that the accused was so disturbed at the time of the attack on Bessie Goodwin that he was incapable of judging "the nature or quality of the act".

Townley's defence was made on the basis of evidence of hereditary insanity within his family – specifically his maternal relatives. This was, at best, a tenuous claim. The only maternal relative to show any signs of mental instability was his grandmother's sister.

This line of defence attracted international interest. In Tasmania, the *Hobart Mercury* discussed the case at length and speculated on the effect that "an eighth or sixteenth of insane blood" might have two generations removed. They appeared to be intrigued by the evidence that prior to 21 August 1863 Townley had shown no signs at all of eccentric behaviour.

Townley's defence tried to build a picture of an unsettled young man. Mr Glover, a bookkeeper who had known Townley for four years was questioned. Glover found him "gentle and reserved in manner" but, significantly extremely exciteable at times. Glover also found Townley prone to despondency.

Three men who had had contact with Townley during his imprisonment were called as witnesses. The Rev. Mr Figgins, Dr Forbes Winslow and the head waiter of the Midland Hotel combined to paint a picture of a "mentally deranged" young man who possessed "a maniacal expression".

Dr Forbes Winslow was of the opinion that Townley's moral compass was more corrupted and impaired than any other person he had met.

Townley appeared to be an atheist. He believed that he was being hounded by five conspirators. He explained his murder of Bessie Goodwin in straightforward terms. She was, effectively, in his mind, the same as his wife. She had committed adultery and he felt that he had the right to take her life. He had the right to reclaim his "property".

The defence called Mr Gisborne, the surgeon at Derby Gaol, and Mr Sims, the Governor. Gisborne felt that Townley was of unsound mind. Sims agreed with the views of Gisborne and Dr Winslow. It was felt that Townley had been consistently strange during his captivity.

Mr Boden, for the prosecution, believed that the evidence of the defence was "totally insufficient". He drew the simple conclusion that if the prisoner knew what he did was against the law and wrong, then he was legally responsible.

Judge Baron Martin was very balanced in his summing up but, ultimately, agreed with the logic of Boden's position. There was no doubt that Townley murdered Bessie Goodwin. The only question was whether he knew what he was doing, or whether he was insane and not responsible for his actions.

The jury returned after only five minutes. The foreman handed in the "Guilty" verdict and the judge donned the black cap to pass a sentence of death.

Sobs and cries were heard in Court. The ladies in the gallery all reached for their handkerchiefs. The prisoner seemed to be the most unconcerned person present.

Townley was told to stand. Whereas for most of the proceedings he had looked at the floor, Townley looked the judge in the eye as the sentence was passed. He then sat down again and resumed his air of indifference. As he was led out of the dock he bowed to the judge "with elegance and grace indicative of polished manners."

George Victor Townley was not to face death on the gallows. The Townley family used their influence to prevail upon the Judge who –

duly – corresponded with Sir George Grey, the Home Secretary.

The law stated that someone sentenced to death could be spared if two Justices of the Peace and two doctors certified that the person was insane. The Townley family held the view that George was now insane – even though he may not have been at the time he committed the murder.

The case was prepared and the evidence put before Sir George Grey. Townley, after much consideration, was declared sane, The Home Secretary upheld the death penalty – but, commuted it to penal servitude for life.

This sequence of events was not universally well-received. Many criticised the actions of the Home Secretary although he certainly acted appropriately and within the law.

It was felt that Townley had cheated the death penalty simply because his family had the means to pay for an expensive private enquiry.

Public opinion on the matter was fuelled by the case of Samuel Wright. He had been tried for the murder of his "paramour" in London at the same time as the Townley case was being debated.

LAMENTATION OF SAMUEL WRIGHT,

Who was Executed on Tuesday, January 12th, 1864, Horsemonger Lane Gaol, for the murder of Eliza Green, on Sunday, 13th of December 1863.

Samuel Wright contemplates George Victor Townley's better fate.

Like Townley, Wright had cut his victim's throat. Like Townley there was some evidence of mental instability. Like Townley there was an approach by men of influence and standing to Sir George Grey. Unlike Townley, Samuel Wright was poor.

The different outcomes of these parallel cases attracted a worldwide interest. The *Otago Witness* newspaper in New Zealand reported the events in January 1864 in great detail.

Sir George Grey's refusal to commute Wright's death penalty prompted a number of large public meetings amongst the working class in Lambeth. Further deputations were sent to the Home Secretary. There was even an approach to Queen Victoria at Windsor. Unfortunately, the Queen's representatives informed Wright's supporters that Her Majesty could only act on the advice of her Ministers.

An M.P. and a local Justice of the Peace had met with the judge before Wright had pleaded guilty and asked him to approach the Home Secretary regarding the case. The judge refused.

The campaign continued at grass roots level until the day of Wright's execution. A handbill, embellished with a black "mourning" border, was circulated :

"A solemn protest against the execution of Wright – men and women of London, abstain from witnessing this sad spectacle of injustice. Let Calcraft and Co. (the executioners) do their work this time with none but the eye of Heaven to look down upon their crime. Let all window shutters be up and all window blinds be down for an hour on Tuesday morning in Southwark. Englishmen, shall Wright be hung? If so, there is one law for thr rich and another for the poor."

The authorities were wary of the public response to Wright's scheduled demise. A substantial force of a thousand Metropolitan Police, some mounted, were held in reserve in the immediate neighbourhood.

They need not have worried. A small crowd gathered to witness Wright's execution – many, perhaps, heeding the sentiments of the handbill.

At 9 a.m. the convict appeared on the scaffold. There were cries of "shame", "bravo Wright" and "God bless you my lad". Two rather more thoughtful shouts were heard – "Judicial Murder" and, tellingly, "Where's Townley ?"

Samuel Wright appeared to be genuinely touched by the level of interest in his fate. He bowed repeatedly in acknowledgement.

The "drop" fell. Wright's end was marked by a roar of indignation.

Later that evening there was yet another well-attended meeting in Lambeth. There was a unanimous vote for the abolition of the death penalty. The "obduracy" of Sir George Grey was debated at some length.

Those present continued to draw stark comparisons between the treatment of Samuel Wright and George Victor Townley. Everyone accepted that both men had "cut the throat of their lady". However, there was a strong feeling that the ingenuity of Townley's solicitor and the unprecedented interference of magistrates and doctors had resulted in his escape from the clutches of the executioner.

George Victor Townley, though, did not appear to welcome the great efforts to save him. He ended his "more humane" sentence on 12 February 1865. He jumped over a staircase railing at Pentonville Prison. Townley was pronounced dead after he fell 23 feet and dashed his skull on the stone floor below.

CHAPTER FOUR
Another Man Scorned

Life's trials and tribulations were never far away in Victorian and Edwardian Derbyshire and inquests were regularly held at the local inn.

The Plough Inn at Brackenfield was to be the scene of two days of dramatic revelations and evidence on 11 May 1896. The Coroner for the Hundred of Scarsdale Mr L Busby had sworn in a jury to conduct the inquest into the violent death of Miss Elizabeth Boot.

The previous Saturday, William Pugh, a twenty-one-year-old unemployed collier from the nearby Shirland Pit, had visited Lindwaylane Farm in Brackenfield. His intention appeared to be either to steal money or, more likely, to do some harm to Lizzie Boot. Lizzie, aged nineteen, was the housekeeper for Mr Thomas Limb who lived at the farm. Mr Limb was away from the farm attending the Matlock May Fair.

It is possible that Pugh had a grudge against Lizzie. Recently, Pugh had attempted to pay court to Lizzie's friend and neighbour, Sarah Saunders. Pugh had boasted that he had £8 to lavish upon Sarah in the hostelries of nearby Alfreton.

Lizzie, though, knew that Pugh was penniless and advised Sarah against taking up with him.

Whatever the actual motive, Pugh visited Lindwaylane Farm and made his way to the barn. Soon afterwards he was seen leaving by a number of witnesses.

A few minutes after Pugh's departure, Lizzie Boot was discovered, lying on her back, with a gash in her throat 5 inches long. The floor of the barn was covered in blood and a blood stained billhook lay discarded nearby.

The Coroner addressed the throng squeezed into the Plough Inn. It was clear that a dreadful crime had been committed. However, even if the jury returned a verdict of murder or manslaughter, he reminded them that a

The Plough Inn, Brackenfield.

trial would follow.

Pugh, by this time, had already been taken into custody. He had been apprehended, ironically, at the neighbouring house where the Saunders family lived. He had blood on his wrists and was nursing a cut over his left eye.

The Coroner took the jury to inspect the barn. The interior had not been cleaned or disturbed. More than one juror was visibly upset by what they had seen.

The proceedings in The Plough Inn had the rapt attention on those assembled. Evidence was given by Lizzie's brother, John Boot. Her seven-year-old-niece Beatrice was called because she was staying with her aunt. She saw Pugh pass through the farmyard and enter the barn. George Hitchcock, farmer from Ashover also saw Pugh.

Harry Towndrow and William Bryan were two farm labourers. They testified that they had seen Pugh spattered with blood and carrying the billhook before returning it to the barn.

Dr Walford from Stonebroom was called to the Plough Inn to present the findings of his post-mortem examination. His precise and scientific account had the clientele of the Plough Inn spellbound:

"I found her a well-nourished young woman. She was lying just as she was found, on her back, her hands were clenched, and her head was turned to the right. There was a large gaping wound in the neck, extending from about an inch and a half to the left of the middle line across to the right to nearly below the ear. The wound sloped slightly upwards to the right. On looking at it closely I found four small cuts where an instrument had cut the skin but not penetrated, just on the edge of the wound. Those cuts corresponded, and showed the gash must have been made by two distinct blows almost in the same spot. The wound had cut though the gullet, severed the air passage, and almost reached the bone. The carotid artery was also severed. On her left hand was a cut two inches long and several others not quite so long …I think it is quite possible that the billhook produced would cause the wounds… Some wounds must have been done by the deceased defending herself. I think she may have been trying to get to the door… I found no signs of outrage on the body and nothing to show that there had been an attempt to commit a rape on the deceased."

(*Derbyshire Times* 13 May 1896)

The gasps which greeted this evidence and the lateness of the hour convinced the Coroner that he should adjourn proceedings until the following morning. The jurors were bound over for the sum of £10 to appear the next day.

A verdict of wilful murder was returned against Pugh following events at the Plough Inn. He was found guilty at the subsequent trial and sentenced to be hanged on Wednesday August 5th.

Pugh, initially, proclaimed his innocence. He wrote some letters – one remarkable example was published in the press:

> To Thos Halsam (Haslam)
> Handicapper
> Shirland
> Near Alfreton
> Derbyshire

From
W Pugh
HM Prison, Derby
May 27th 1896

Dear Friend,

I rite to you hoping to find you in good health that it leaves me very well at present. I want you to remember me to Jack Hoskins and Tom Davis, M Calladine, Moses Rhodes, Sam Blant, Jack Hope,Jack Bramley, Joseph Topham,W Keeton. Tell Tom Davis and Moses Rhodes its not a bad stall the coal gets pretty well we don't want any holing doing.

Rite back and tell me how you are getting on at pit. God bless you all the Assize is on the tenth of July then we shall (know) more than we do now.

I should like to see you there because I think well of you Tommie and Tom Davis so God bless you and your wives and your family your loving friend William Pugh.

Yea though I walk through the valley of the shadows of death I will fear no evil:for thou art with me:thy rod and thy staff they comfort me.

A collier chap black on the skin;

But whiter far he lies within;

The Holy Trinity Church Brackenfield.

Lizzie Boot still remembered in the Holy Trinity Church Brackenfield.

Lizzie Boot's memorial at Holy Trinity Brackenfield.

This secret now the Collier doth know
They think I am as black as hell but white as snow;
Water will was and cleanse the skin
But oh his blood must cleanse within;
That blood which ran on calvary's hill;
Though but a collier was shed for me
Rite back Tommie and tell me how they are all getting on your loving friend William Pugh.

William Pugh
HM Prison
Derby "

(*Derbyshire Times* Saturday 6 June 1896)

Pugh made a full confession on the morning of his execution. He walked to the scaffold quietly after enjoying a good breakfast. A large crowd of two thousand had gathered outside Derby Gaol to witness the hoisting of the black flag. Billington was the executioner and he carried out the sentence at ten minutes past eight. Death was instantaneous.

Locally, the scene of the murder attracted great interest. Claims that the barn was haunted did little to stem the flow of ghoulish sightseers.

Lindwaylane Farm was visited by more than three thousand people following the Plough Inn inquest. Many were accommodated in local farms and hostelries.

More than a dozen "brakes and traps" were to be seen ferrying visitors from Alfreton and other neighbouring towns.

The site itself may have proved a little disappointing for some later arrivals. The top door of the barn and a brick from the wall which had traces of blood and hair had been removed by the Police.

The wooden floor upon which Lizzie Boot had been discovered had been removed, bit by bit, by souvenir hunters.

Mr Limb, retrospectively, levied a charge for entrance to the barn. A sum of about £11 in coppers was given for a memorial stone for Lizzie Boot in the churchyard of the Holy Trinity church at Brackenfield.

CHAPTER FIVE

A Victorian General Election –
a Riot in Clay Cross!

In November 1868 Britain was in the grip of election fever. William Gladstone's Liberal Party were locked in a battle with Benjamin Disraeli's Conservatives.

In Clay Cross a large gathering of local colliers, young and old, sporting the "yellow" colours of the more "radical" Liberal Party were agitated. Rumours were circulating that the two Conservative candidates were currently leading in the poll.

A gentleman believed to be a Conservative candidate was pelted with stones and narrowly avoided serious injury. Soon afterwards the Rev. J. Nodder, the Rector of Ashover, appeared in his carriage sporting "blue" Conservative favours. This proved unwise.

The clergyman, a very prominent local figure, was bombarded with missiles from all sides. The Rev. Nodder quickly took refuge in the Public Hall. He was then spirited out of the building by some "radicals" who seemed to have some influence with the baying crowd outside.

The mob, having been disappointed in pursuit of the original quarry, had to be content with attacking any carriage decked in "blue" ribbons.

The violence escalated to such an extent that, by the afternoon, fifty constables from the Birmingham Borough Police Force were required to assist the twenty members of the Derbyshire County Constabulary already on duty. The constables used their staves robustly. Unfortunately, a woman had her arm broken and this prompted even more stone throwing.

Charles Binns, the manager of the Clay Cross Coal and Iron Works and who lived at Clay Cross Hall, had some influence with the mob. He bravely faced the crowd as stones flew in every direction. Exasperated, he eventually ran towards a ringleader who responded by attempting to

In 1868 this was the New Inn in Clay Cross.

Sir Joshua Walmsley in 1871.

strike Binns with some force. Binns was carried to comparative safety and placed on top of a wall where he appealed for calm. This worked – but only for a short while.

The Public Hall, in which the Police were based, came under sustained attack. Conservative posting boards were dismantled and used as weapons in an assault on the New Inn.

The New Inn was targeted because it was the location of a Conservative Committee Room. Inspector Fearn, a gentleman charged with quelling the disturbance, was approaching the public house as it became the main target. He must have felt vulnerable as all the windows were smashed with "stones and brick end going in like hail".

Fearn was more fortunate than Henry Hall. He was a clerk to the Conservatives and was hit on the back of the head – he had difficulty shielding himself as he had only one arm. Witnesses saw him fall to the floor "as if dead".

The Star Inn was next public house to be attacked. All the windows were quickly smashed. A neighbouring house belonging to Samuel Dore was attacked with its windows also being "put in by a combination of stones and props". Mr Udall, the local draper, saw his property suffer a similar fate.

Meanwhile, the unfortunate Rev. Nodder was finally cornered. His carriage was "smashed to atoms" with the remnants thrown in a field next to the Shakespeare Inn.

The Queen's Hotel was next to feel the force of the mob – being identified as a "Conservative house". Every pane of glass was broken and during this attack three milk churns were used as missiles as stones were now in short supply.

A large stone narrowly missed Mrs Dore, the wife of the owner – embedding itself two inches into the wall. One large pole – "four yards long and four inches square" – was dispatched through a passage window. Mr Dore, was relieved that he had sent his two children to safety as their room was soon littered with debris.

Two more public houses suffered damage as the mob roamed around Clay Cross. The Prince of Wales and The Buck were next, the latter joining others in having all its windows smashed.

The sound of breaking glass was not restricted to public houses. Inspector Fearn's home and the butcher's shop of William Slack were soon involved.

Mr Cresswell's property not only had its windows destroyed but also much of his "woodwork". He received special treatment because he had been responsible for the Conservative Party's bill posting.

The study of the local curate, Rev. T. Oldham, was a target but, at least, here the Police managed to apprehend two ringleaders and put them in the "lock-up".

The day saw more attacks, with the shops of Mr Bradley, a wheelwright, and Mr Wilson, a "druggist", falling victim.

Mr Leafe, a grocer, unlike the other businessmen was not intending to vote in 1868. His property was attacked anyway !

If Mr Leafe could count himself very unlucky then Mr Holdsworth was truly the opposite. He was a leading Conservative and proprietor of the Clay Cross Company. His house was identified by the mob as another prime target but, at the last minute, it was pacified by a Colliery Superintendant who reported Holdsworth had, that very morning, turned from a "blue" to a "yellow"!

The prominent Liberal politician, Sir Joshua Walmsley, who was in North Derbyshire for the election, went in to the crowd at Clay Cross to appeal for calm. Walmsley was very well respected and had an affinity with the area. He had worked with George Stephenson whose railway and colliery initiatives had been instrumental in the development of the industrial community of Clay Cross. He was also an influential figure in the "national reform movement".

Sir Joshua made it clear that he disapproved of the actions of a large number of Clay Cross residents. He appeared to strike a chord and, by midnight, the worst of the disorder was over and the streets were reported as being "pretty clear".

Throughout the day in Clay Cross, voters had been asked at the polling booths whether they were "blues" or "yellows" – if they replied the former they were "driven back".

Francis Egerton and Henry Strutt were duly elected as Members of Parliament. They were Liberals ("yellow") and represented the large East Derbyshire constituency which included Clay Cross.

On 3 December 1868, William Ewart Gladstone, the leader of the Liberal Party, had his first audience as Prime Minister with Queen Victoria at Windsor.

CHAPTER SIX
An Unfortunate Walk in the Peak

In the Autumn of 1900 Derbyshire folk were fascinated with events in, and around, the picturesque Peak District village of Beeley. Interest was focussed on the disappearance of Mary Ann Elliott and the behaviour of her husband William.

A number of witnesses reported seeing Mary Ann loitering outside the Square and Compass Inn at Darley Bridge on Saturday 27th October. She had clearly been drinking and, from time to time, she entered the premises to seek out William Elliott.

Mary Ann was keen for them to move on. On one occasion she was seen to actually poke her husband with a stick in the hope of extracting him from the comfort of his surroundings. William had been in the Square and Compass for a few hours having successfully traded some fowls to his fellow customers.

P.C. Rowlett was on duty at Darley Bridge and came across Mary Ann. He was concerned about her demeanour. He noticed she was smartly dressed. She had a watch and chain and was wearing a shawl around her neck. Mary Ann was looking in her purse which seemed to contain a number of coins.

Rowlett encouraged a small group of youths to move on before he entered the Square and Compass to enquire if anyone knew Mary Ann. Once inside he was soon informed that she was "Bint's wife" – William Elliott was known to locals as "Bint".

Rowlett asked Elliott to leave the Square and Compass and ensure that Mary Ann was safely escorted home – otherwise he would be forced to "lock her up" as she was under the influence of drink.

The Elliotts were observed leaving Darley Bridge and heading off in the direction of Beeley where their small cottage was situated.

Beeley – the home of the Elliotts.

Opposite, top: *The Square and Compass – events began here.*
bottom: *The Grouse Inn – the body of Mary Ann Elliott was taken here.*

On the way William Elliott called briefly at the Church Inn and, afterwards, attempted to enter The Grouse. However, the diligent P.C. Rowlett had followed the pair and refused William entry saying that he had already "had enough".

The Elliotts were having words. William was quite a distance in front of Mary Ann as they were last seen together at Rowsley before taking the turning for Beeley. P.C. Rowlett watched them disappear into the distance confident that Mary Ann seemed likely to follow her husband the remainder of the way home.

We know that William Elliott arrived home, in a drunken state, just after midnight. His four children and Mary Ann's fifteen-year-old sister Esther Stone were asleep. The eldest of the children was aged ten and all the family slept in the one bedroom.

Esther heard William come in and enquired about the whereabouts of Mary Ann. William told her that she was not in. He then sexually assaulted Esther despite her requests for him to "go away" and knowing that she was only fifteen.

Esther later was to testify that this was the second occasion that Elliott had done this.

William Elliott was charged with the assault just as investigations into the disappearance of Mary Ann Elliott were beginning.

"The Beeley Mystery" was gathering momentum as speculation about Mrs Elliott was rife. The news about the assault on Esther Stone merely served to feed the frenzied level of interest. Many believed that Mary Ann had planned her disappearance to escape an unhappy marriage – it was known that William had beaten her in the past. This, they thought, would explain her "best" dress and the amount of money she was supposedly carrying in her purse.

However, many others maintained that, although there was a history of violence in the Elliott's marriage, they were actually often happy together. Indeed, on the night of her disappearance Mary Ann seemed determined to follow her husband for some considerable distance.

Part of the mystery was solved a few weeks after that fateful night in Darley Bridge. The body of a woman was found in a pond on the Stancliffe Estates very close to where Mary Ann was last seen alive. The body was taken to the Grouse Inn where it was identified as that of Mary Ann Elliott.

The inquest was held at the Grouse. The Coroner heard that the body of Mrs Elliott was partially clothed. Her dress skirt and her hat were found in trees and shrubs nearby. It was noted that the "hat pins are drawn as if the hat had been carefully removed." Likewise, the hooks and eyes of the dress were all in good order.

Theft appeared not to be a motive behind any foul deed. A purse was found in the pocket of the dress which contained a number of coins, including a florin. There was also a wedding ring and a key. Mary Ann was still wearing her wedding ring.

The post-mortem examination revealed no marks or injuries which would account for her death. Indeed, "a large piece of mud" in her mouth indicated that Mary Ann may have been alive as she entered the water.

The Coroner decided that the cause of death was drowning. He then considered some different scenarios which could have led to this outcome.

Had Mary Ann simply become exhausted and simply bedded down for the night ? Then, intoxicated, had she slid into the pond accidentally ?

A second possibility, the Coroner said, was that she was afraid of going home with William and decided to end her own life.

A third possibility was that there was some other person involved. The obvious candidate was her husband, according to the Coroner :

"He had ill-used her and threatened to ill-use her again. On this very night they were not on good terms. When he left her close to this place about 11 o'clock at night he did not go to Beeley for something like two hours after. There is a very considerable space of time not accounted for. "

Surprisingly, the Coroner decided it wasn't worth adjourning the inquest to fetch William Elliott back from Derby Gaol. It was there that he was serving nine months hard labour for his assault on Esther Stone. He was dismissive of William Elliott's likely contribution :

"Personally, I do not think it will be worth it, because I say if the man comes, from what I hear of his condition, he would not be of the slightest use to us."

The jury did not even leave the room and after "a minute or two" of conversation returned the open verdict – "found drowned, and there is not sufficient evidence to show how she came into the water."

CHAPTER SEVEN

Velocipedes – Fashionable and Fast in Derbyshire!

In July 1869 a national craze was to make its impact on Derbyshire. A four-wheeled contraption was being propelled at some speed down the hill past the Royal Oak public house at Old Tupton. The four passengers were to be thrown out as it overturned – one of them, Mr Smith, was seriously injured.

The vehicle involved was a velocipede. It was an early form of bicycle which was made of iron and wood. They were driven forward by pedalling cranks on the front axle and had become popular again following improvements in design made by the Michaux family in Paris. Missing from their design was any form of spring or suspension and this deficiency gave rise to the nickname – "boneshaker".

The Royal Oak example was certainly not one of the refined French versions designed for solo use. It was a larger version built by employees of a Mr Rooth in Chesterfield. The four-wheel design was similar to one involved in a fatal accident in Newcastle a few months previously – a seventy-eight-year-old woman had been mown down by four gentlemen in the North East. The gentlemen in question were charged with "culpably and recklessly" causing the death of the lady.

The city of Derby had also witnessed a serious incident. William Chapman, a labourer, became a victim of "velocipede road rage".

Chapman had enjoyed an evening at the Barley Mow at Litchurch when he, rashly, spread his arms to attempt to slow down two speeding machines. His intervention caused the second velocipede to swerve and hit some railings at the roadside.

A violent confrontation ensued and Chapman was struck repeatedly by one of the aggrieved cyclists. He subsequently died.

The Coroner seemed to have little sympathy with Chapman's objection to the speed of the velocipedes. In his summing up he said – "If two men went voluntarily into battle, and one was killed, it was manslaughter. Of course, it was absurd to say one word as to any charge of murder. It was evident that Chapman was in liquor, and he had no right to interrupt or abuse anybody on the road."

Chapman's assailant was acquitted, there were doubts as to exactly how his fatal "concussion of the brain" had been caused.

Velocipede riding in Derbyshire was clearly becoming both popular and risky. In September 1869 a group of people from Buxton had a lucky escape.

Two gentlemen decided to make the journey from Buxton to Whaley Bridge and Disley via velocipede. The wife of one of the gentlemen travelled ahead by rail but met up with them at Disley where they all enjoyed a day at the agricultural show.

They accumulated a rather "corpulent" gentleman who, apparently, gloried in the name of "John Barleycorn". He invited himself back on their return journey – which they began rather late in the evening with the lady preferring to walk alongside the velocipede.

Darkness, rain and the inevitable steep hill caused the small party to halt. John Barleycorn proved to be merely a burden as he, stubbornly, refused to dismount and assist. Luckily, the only female present showed great initiative and resolve.

She used some harnessing and yoked herself to the velocipede …and its weighty passenger. She "pulled with a will" and managed to arrive at the top of the hill. The gentlemen then, rather ungallantly, climbed aboard and sped off at great pace towards Buxton with John Barleycorn at the helm.

For half a mile it was exhilarating and fun. However, the

An old postcard showing the dangers of velocipede racing.

velocipede left the road and struck a wall with some force. Amazingly, no-one was seriously injured but the velocipede was in a sorry state. The front wheels had parted company with the frame which was bent into "beautifully artistic shapes".

John Barleycorn was never seen again – some thought he was worried that he would be blamed for the catastrophe.

Velocipedes had clearly gripped the nation and Derbyshire was to provide further evidence of their more enjoyable and sporting impact.

In August 1869 a Grand Picnic and Gala took place at Ashover on lands owned by the Reverend J. Nutter to raise funds for the Brampton Cricket Club and the local museum. There was grand entertainment to match the beautiful weather.

The Chesterfield Volunteer Band led a procession of carriages and games of cricket and croquet were enjoyed by many. Dancing, fireworks and" fire balloons" occupied the crowds drawn from Clay Cross, Ashover, Matlock, Tupton and Holymoorside. The main attraction, though, was a series of velocipede races – Ashover was keen to join Chesterfield in

The slope in Tupton.

44

recognising this craze. Chesterfield had already hosted such races in May 1869 as part of athletics meetings. The velocipede events were the most expensive to watch and winners were rewarded with the highest prize money. The events at Brampton were only open to professionals.

The summer gathering at Ashover was to be treated to a demonstration of some "daredevil" feats by Mr Brown – himself a professional exponent of the velocipede. It was fashionable at the time to engage such riders who claimed to be "artists who draw a four wheel cab, containing four persons, run up an incline, leap twelve feet into the air whilst on the velocipede". Chairs, bottles and cans featured as props as did boasts of the ability to transport six men at once.

Fittingly, the best amateur at the Ashover Grand Picnic and Gala was the local man Mr W Marshall who won a series of races and duly carried off the winner's Silver Cup. Mr. Marshall, who lived in Wingerworth, was evidently very keen and talented. He had also seen off fellow competitors at the Bolsover Races a fortnight previously.

Interestingly, at Ashover the more sedate control of a velocipede was clearly recognised because Mr W.A. Stamford won a prize for his slow riding!

The emergence of the velocipede provoked a great deal of debate. Many saw it filling a gap in available transport, one keen advocate observing – " it's utility consists of it being a go-between riding and walking; it enables you to see and get about the country, free from all care or expense; it is immeasurably superior to walking, and yet not equal, for ease – to horse carriage."

French magazines continued to champion the velocipede and suggest many different uses – amusingly, the conduct of funerals. However, like all crazes, fascination with the velocipede was to peak in 1869 and fade quickly afterwards.

The quest for more efficiency in respect of distance travelled led to the front wheels becoming larger and larger – until the more familiar "penny farthing" design soon emerged.

However, for a short period Derbyshire was very much in touch with a fashionable sporting trend.

CHAPTER EIGHT

Victorian Inns – Derbyshire Life Through the Keyhole

A local flower show and a red rose triggered a violent episode in the Greyhound Inn at Dronfield in October 1890.

George Wilson, a local man, had been to Dronfield Flower Show and had called at the Greyhound with his brother-in-law John Cartledge who was a farmer from nearby Intake. Wilson ordered some ale and was served by Caroline Daisley. He paid with one shilling and Daisley had to go and find some change.

The ownership of a rather fine red rose was then the cause of a dispute between Wilson and another drinker – William Hawkins. Wilson and Hawkins both claimed that the other had snatched the rose, although it is probable that the rose belonged to Wilson.

An argument developed into a fight in the kitchen after the landlord, Thomas Burley, claimed he had attempted to evict Wilson and Cartledge from the premises.

Caroline Daisley entered the kitchen with Wilson's change. At this point she saw Hawkins hit Wilson. Cartledge was trying to intervene when Daisley picked up a fire shovel and came at him yelling "I'll clear thee out" before hitting Cartledge over the eye and "cutting it out".

 Cartledge said that he was merely attempting to split the protagonists up. He claimed that he had no dispute with anyone but had been knocked senseless. The unfortunate man only regained consciousness as he was bundled into a waggonette to be taken for treatment. His right eye was totally destroyed.

Doctor John Mackensie from Intake, who examined Cartledge and who gave evidence at the subsequent trial, confirmed the nature of the injury – " an angular wound to the right eye, the short angle being lacerated. The wound could be caused by a blow from an ordinary fire shovel. The sight

Life played out in streets like this.

was entirely gone."

Witnesses were called and Ella Stemson said that she saw the blow and heard Daisley say something like "take the sen out!"

Proceedings were compromised when a lodger at the Greyhound gave a different version of events.

William Thompson, a miner from Liverpool, said that Wilson and Hawkins were indeed fighting, but Cartledge played a more active role than he had claimed. Thompson said that Cartledge had struck both himself and the landlord.

Thompson went on to say that he had "brodged" Cartledge in the eye with "something" he picked up in the struggle. Thompson said he had to take some action otherwise he would have had "his head knocked off".

Thompson said that Cartledge was drunk and hit Daisley "as you would hit a man".

The charges against Wilson and Cartledge for refusing to leave the

Greyhound were dropped. Caroline Daisley was found guilty of a common assault. The Bench had decided to reduce the charge from a more serious "indictable" offence but was resolved to give a "warning to her and others that they could not arm themselves with fire shovels and strike a man in the way the complainant had been struck." Daisley was fined £3 plus costs or, as an alternative, one months hard labour.

In September 1900 the eyesight of another victim was to be damaged during an incident at a Derbyshire inn.

Henry Smith was holding a horse and trap outside The Crown Hotel in Tibshelf. Henry, already, only had the sight of his left eye following an accident in the pit in 1885. He had received treatment but had been unable to work since and resided at the Belper Union.

Unfortunately for Smith, Bill White of Tibshelf mistook misfortune for idleness. White had made it plain to the regulars in the Crown that he was going to assault Smith when he next saw him – even though he had never had a conversation with him and did not know him.

Hence, as Smith was holding the horse and trap White came up behind him and pulled him around by the right shoulder and hit him hard in the right eye. Smith fell to the ground and, as he tried to get to his feet, was knocked down again.

Witnesses heard White say "Get up and I will serve you the same again!" The dazed Smith replied "I can't – you have blinded me !"

Witnesses told White that he ought to be ashamed of himself but he attempted to justify his actions by proclaiming – "that is how all such want serving".

White realised that he may have gone too far and took himself off to Warsop near Mansfield. He was arrested ten months later, at 7a.m on 22 August 1900 by P.C. Bown. When cornered White made the simple statement – " I have nothing to say".

Sadly, the victim of the attack was forced to live in Derby Infirmary. Dr Vernon Bensley who treated the unfortunate Henry Smith confirmed that, although he could tell light from dark, his sight would never improve.

In October 1900 William White was sentenced to twelve months by the judge who commented that "a worse case of cowardly and ruffianly assault he had never listened to."

In the summer of the same year, William Green, the landlord of the Miners Arms in Newbold, found himself in court. He was charged with twelve specific indictments of using his licensed premises for the purpose of betting.

William Green was well known locally as a "bookmaker". People often visited the Miners Arms and placed bets either with the landlord or his brother, Charles. Charles Green also ended up in court charged with aiding and abetting the illegal practices.

Things were going swimmingly until Whit Monday which fell on 4 June. Fanny White, a regular at the pub, called in to claim her winnings of £6 15s. This was a considerable sum and had been won as the result of a rather fortunate sequence of results on her "accumulator" bet.

William Green refused to pay out. Mr White very rapidly arrived at the Miners Arms and demanded his wife's winnings. The Greens still refused to pay.

Mr White refused to leave the premises until he received the £6 15s. The Police were called as Mr White was guilty of "refusal to quit a Public House".

The arrival of the Police gave Mr White the opportunity to share with the authorities his considerable knowledge of illegal gambling activity at the Miners Arms. Only a few days before, on 30 May, he had backed "Forfarshire" in the Derby for 10s and lost. The following day he had

The Crown Hotel, Tibshelf.

placed another 10s on "Winifreda" in the Oaks and lost again. On 2nd June, in determined fashion he had placed 10s on "School Girl" in another race and lost again. However, a second bet that day on a horse called "Blacksmith" finally paid dividends. Charles Green paid him 8s 4d.

On 4 June Mrs White had made four bets. The details were written on a piece of paper which was delivered to the Miners Arms, along with the correct stake money, by a lady friend of Fanny White.

William Green had explained to the Whites that he could not find the piece of paper. He also antagonised them further by reminding them that betting money could not be recovered because the entire transaction was illegal anyway !

In court Alderman Johnson Pearson tried to make some sense of the situation. He asked White if he himself had ever been a landlord. White replied that he had. Pearson's line of argument was developed when Mr A. Muir Wilson, who was defending Green, asked –

"And you know betting in a public house was punishable with a fine?"

"Yes it is" replied Mr White "…if you get catched."

At this point those present in the courtroom burst into laughter.

Green stated that he had paid Mrs White some money even though he couldn't find the original paper so the bet was off. He paid her 2s 7d as a result of the first three bets she claimed she had made. He was unwilling to pay out the larger sum from her "accumulator".

Fanny White was called to give evidence and reduced the courtroom to laughter again when she confirmed that, had Green paid out, Mr White would never have known about the bet at all!

Mr A. Muir Wilson, summing up on behalf of Mr Green, called Mr White a "sneak". He said that White had only reported Green's betting sideline when it became clear that he wasn't going to be satisfied over the payment of his wife's wager. He went on to say that,as a former, publican White knew full well what was going on and what was at stake.

Muir Wilson concluded by saying about Mr White – "If he lived amongst honourable British subjects they would give him a good hiding when he got home."

Green admitted making three bets illegally but had "honestly" paid out 2s 7d. He denied attempting to "bounce" Fanny White out of the sum of £6 15s.

A plea was made on behalf of Green. The Tadcaster Brewery Company could evict him from the Miners Arms within seven days under the terms of their arrangement.

The court was made aware that Fanny White "had a knowledge of betting that was remarkable in a woman." An interesting insight into the social attitudes of the time !

Green was fined £10 for the gambling offences on the previous Whit Monday. However, his license was not affected. All other charges were withdrawn, including all those against Charles Green.

A pleasant, warm day provided the ideal backdrop for opportunism and alcohol to combine outside the Royal Oak at Old Tupton in 1887.

Samuel Gascoyne was employed as a cab driver by Mr T. Paulson of Chesterfield. He was transporting Mr Curtis along the road from Derby when his passenger suggested rest and refreshment at the Royal Oak. The problem of tending the cab was solved by an obliging bystander – James Sheriffe who was provided with a beer for his trouble.

Gascoyne and Mr Curtis re-emerged from the public house to discover that the rather fine horse and cab had disappeared – as had James Sheriffe!

P.C. Clarke was alerted and set off in pursuit, correctly guessing that Sheriffe had taken off in the direction of Chesterfield. Numerous sightings were to follow in Chesterfield, Ashover, Kelstedge, Cromford, Wirksworth and Duffield.

At one point Sheriffe had actually been accompanied up Slack Hill near Kelstedge by George Thompson who was the local policeman. The latter, although not perceptive enough to realise that he was in the company of a felon did recognise the horse. Thompson correctly identified, in jolly conversation with Sheriffe, that the unfortunate and weary beast had once belonged to Dr Lee from Clay Cross.

After a considerable tour of Derbyshire the horse and cab were discovered abandoned near Duffield. John Cooper and William Askew were on their way to work when they came across the cab turned over at the roadside. The horse was still in the shafts, wet with sweat but trembling and cold. It was exhausted and had clearly travelled a number of miles.

Cooper and Askew dutifully took the horse and cab to the County Police Office in Derby. James Sheriffe was arrested at Derby Workhouse despite his spirited denial – "I know nothing about it, I'm innocent enough."

Sheriffe claimed that he had been having a nap under a wall when the cab had passed him near the blacksmith's shop at Tupton. He said that he had walked all the way to Derby apart from the stretch from Higham to Ambergate when he was given a ride by "a man he did not know".

Eventually the thirty-one-year-old Sheriffe admitted stealing a horse, a hansom cab, and a set of harness belonging to Thomas Paulson of Chesterfield. The value of Paulson's property was estimated at the considerable sum of £50.

James Sheriffe "begged pardon" for the crime. He admitted that he was very drunk at the time. He explained that, having suffered from sunstroke whilst in India, he could never remember what he did when intoxicated.

The Court took a rather dim view of Sheriffe's actions and was not influenced greatly by the fact that all the property, save the harness, had been recovered.

It was not the first occasion that Sheriffe's excessive consumption of beer had landed him in trouble with the authorities. Magistrates had often found it their "painful duty" to sentence him to "various terms of imprisonment."

His Lordship, on this occasion, decided that the sentence should not only punish Sheriffe, but also offer the opportunity to help him live without drink. It was decided that for his own sake and for the sake of the public he should serve nine months imprisonment with hard labour.

This sentence was designed to cure Sheriffe's devotion to drink and prevent his assaults on his neighbours and the police. His Lordship also believed that his obscene use of language would be checked – as this was linked to his beer consumption.

His Lordship concluded by saying that he had no doubt that when Sheriffe came out he would have discovered "how wonderfully well he could live without drink".

CHAPTER NINE
Suffer Little Children

Few crimes exercise the public imagination more than a mother murdering her children. Add an insurance pay-out and an attempted suicide in Victorian England and you have a truly combustible situation.

In November 1887 the Whitfield family came to live in the parish of Hasland near Chesterfield. John Whitfield was an engine driver and Mary Whitfield looked after their four children in Whitebank Yard.

Neighbours remember the Whitfield children as being "all perfectly healthy" when the family set up home. However, in June 1888 young Alfred Whitfield began to feel ill and needed to be seen by the doctor. The treatments prescribed had no effect and on 10 June Alfred died.

Later in June, Alfred's eight-year-old brother, Ernest, began to present similar symptoms. He had difficulty controlling his limbs, was struggling to breathe and began to choke.

Initially neighbours attempted to help. Mary Whitfield kept laudanum in the house and they saw her offer some to the ailing Ernest who was reluctant to drink it, muttering "not that stuff!" Mary drank some herself.

Mrs Whitfield had passed out and was on the floor by the time Doctor Shea arrived. Ernest, by this time, was also in a state of collapse. He died in the early hours of the following morning.

The sudden deaths of the two young brothers, so close together, caused concern. This hardened into suspicion when Mr Whitfield fell ill with similar, though milder, symptoms.

Soon after Ernest's death, Mary Whitfield had tried to borrow money from her neighbours saying that her husband was off work and that his clothes were "in pawn". The neighbours refused to lend her any money and Mrs Whitfield replied "well, it's an off-day tomorrow he'll have to be a prisoner !"

John Whitfield continued to be a "prisoner" and was confined to the family home. He seemed to be losing the use of his legs.

At Christmas 1888, Mr Whitfield was still housebound and Mary, obviously keen to mark the season, commented to a neighbour "I have threepence, I will get him a pint of beer and give him a sweat."

Financially, Mrs Whitfield had seen some improvement. At the end of 1887 she had insured the lives of all her children. On the death of Alfred the Wesleyan and General Insurance Company had paid out £10 6s. The premium on Ernest's policy was 1d per week and £4 was to be paid out if he died after four months. However, if he lived for six months from the start of the policy the pay-out would increase to £6. Ernest survived for six months – exactly.

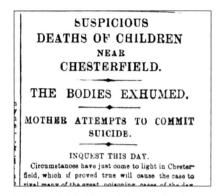

Mary Whitfield headline Derbyshire Times *20 February 1889.*

On 4 February 1889, Mary Whitfield attempted suicide by taking opium. Her symptoms were similar to Alfred's and Ernest's and, to a lesser extent those of John Whitfield.

Mary's attempt at suicide was a criminal offence. She was taken into custody. Immediately, John Whitfield began to recover and the long-harboured suspicions came to the fore.

Mary Whitfield stood trial at the Derbyshire Summer Assizes. She faced two charges, the wilful murder of her son Ernest at Hasland in June 1888 and attempting suicide in February 1889.

The courtroom was packed. Mary Whitfield, wearing a black bonnet and checked shawl, answered the charges in a soft voice – "not guilty".

Sir Henry Hawkins, presiding, kindly allowed Mrs Whitfield to sit saying he "did not think they ought to keep any prisoner standing".

Crowds had gathered and followed Mary Whitfield at numerous adjournments. Large numbers of people waited at Chesterfield railway station as she was transported from Derby Gaol. Everyone was eager to catch even the most fleeting glimpse of her as she was quickly escorted into a cab for the short journey to the Magistrates' Clerk's office on West Bars.

The case against Mary Whitfield had its focus on Ernest and not Alfred for scientific reasons. The bodies of the boys had been dramatically exhumed from Hasland Cemetery. Ernest's body was the much better preserved of the two and, amazingly, still had traces of opium present.

The evidence presented at the trial as damning. Neighbours described symptoms which would point to poisoning by laudanum and opium.

Mary Simpson, a neighbour, had accompanied Mary Whitfield to the insurance offices after Alfred's death. She testified that two advances of money were paid. She also said that Mary was drunk at Alfred's funeral.

In her defence, Mrs Whitfield blamed Ernest's death on him catching a chill following paddling in the local brook. She admitted being drunk at Ernest's funeral.

Mrs Whitfield, though, had an able and articulate defender in her legal counsel, Mr Hextall. He did not dispute the fact that Mary had purchased laudanum or that she had it in the house. Instead, Hextall pointed out that not one witness had actually seen it administered to the boys in large doses.

The remaining terraced housing where the Whitfields once lived.

Hextall then played his ace card. He questioned whether any mother would be callous enough to murder two of her children. He pointed out that Mrs Whitfield's dealings with the insurance company were very public and entirely legal.

He went on to say that the "considerable" evidence for the prosecution was, in fact, wholly circumstantial. In spoke for more than one and three quarter hours and in conclusion said:

"Remember gentlemen, that on the verdict you give hangs not only this life of this poor woman; remember that, although two children of her have died, there is left to her two others alive and well, and who await with trembling anxiety the verdict you arrive at. I hope and trust the verdict will be one of "not guilty", and one which will restore to them the person who, however wanting she may have been in some respects, however badly she may have fulfilled duties she might have fulfilled better, was at least to her husband, a wife, and to her children, a mother."

The judge completed his summing up and the jury were sent out to consider their verdict. They deliberated for fifty-five minutes before returning.

Mary Whitfield had to be helped up the steps and looked ill as she "staggered to the front of the dock".

She clutched the rail. The Clerk of the Court asked the foreman if they had agreed on a verdict. The foreman replied that they had and it was – "not guilty".

The verdict was greeted with shock. Those inside the court were stunned – the defendant appeared equally surprised.

The crowd outside the court was confused as the news filtered through. Later, the *Derbyshire Times* commented that the verdict "was received with almost universal indignation, and when it was announced in our special editions, in the very short time after its pronunciation the general belief was that a mistake must have occurred in transmission."

Mary Whitfield did not quite walk free. She was sentenced to four months hard labour for her attempted suicide.

CHAPTER TEN

Giving the Olympians a Run for their Money!

It was the summer of 1869. In France, a young Pierre de Coubertain was eagerly reading British adventure stories which glorified physical fitness and strength. In Britain those very attributes were being supported and celebrated in …Brampton!

In June 1869 "The Brampton Athletic Sports" took place behind the Britannia Inn. The weather was fine – numerous entries and a large crowd combined to make it a great success.

The Brampton event was typical of its time. It began with a Handicap Walking Race which was won by W. Wall of Ridgeway who "wore an exceedingly neat costume" !

Handicapping and appearance were important features of the day. The walking race was followed by the Handicap Flat Race of 120 yards which was won by J. Milner of Sheffield. The Hurdle Handicap Race, which followed, proved to be no obstacle to G. Stanton of Chesterfield. He safely negotiated the 300 yards and six hurdles.

A parade was held, after the "blue riband" athletics events, to enable the smartness of competitors to be judged. It was clearly an inclusive event – an eight-year-old boy claimed the second prize.

Next was a Running High Jump in which J. Musgrove of Belper demonstrated "some beautiful leaping" upon clearing 5 feet.

Brampton, like the modern Olympics today, had its specialist disciplines. Throwing the cricket ball was routinely won by J. Simpson of Chesterfield but the "Fifty Pot Nurs" caused consternation and distress amongst participants.

In this, competitors had to run to pick up a small round ball and return it to a basket at the starting point. The fifty "nurs" were placed one yard apart meaning that the runners had to travel more than a mile in total, and

The Britannia Inn, Brampton.

at some pace. They also had to stop – and stoop – fifty times.

Cycling also featured – early "bone shaker" velocipedes being the means of transport. The newly formed Amateur Athletics Club, who thought any physical reward or payment for victors was unnecessary, would have been disappointed with Mr J. Cooper of Manchester. He carried off a "handsome timepiece" for winning.

The runner-up may have shared some sense of disappointment with the Amateur Athletics Club – but for a different reason. He won a coffee service.

The Britannia Inn at Brampton was joined by its namesake in Tupton which hosted the gloriously named "All England Handicap" in August. This race, over 130 yards, was sponsored by Messrs W. Holmes and J. Metcalf for the considerable sum of £3. The Amateur Athletics Club still, clearly, had some arguments to win in North Derbyshire !

The Tupton event was also very well attended despite an admission fee of 1s 6d. A high standard of dress was again expected. The runners were instructed to compete in "long drawers and singlets".

The race proved to be a thriller – J. Lowther from Seymour saw off his two close Clay Cross challengers J. Evans and G. Beastall by a matter of feet. He carried off the winner's prize of £2 – Evans earned himself 15s and the poor, exhausted Beastall just 5s!

Nearby a rather more violent sporting event was taking place. At the Royal Oak in Tupton the princely sum of £5 was the prize in a "catch as catch can" wrestling bout.

"Little Walley" of Clay Cross was matched against "Big George" (alias the "Bull Stirk") of Tupton. Names proved deceptive as "Little Walley" threw his opponent very easily ...twice !

The small crowd was disappointed with the rapid conclusion – but was promised a re-match as soon as "Big George" had recovered.

At least Little Walley didn't end up in front of the Magistrates – a fate which befell some Staveley prizefighters.

James Bower (alias "Swaddy Bower"), James Clarke ("London

The Britannia Inn, Tupton.

Victorian prizefighters.

Jimmy"), and James Parsons ("Lemonade Jimmy") were charged with committing a breach of the peace.

Names, again, were deceptive. "Lemonade Jimmy" thought he had killed "London Jimmy" who, after a fight lasting one hour and thirty-three minutes, had difficulty dragging himself off the grass. A crowd of two hundred were present around the ring which was maintained by a man wielding a hedge stake in the absence of proper ropes.

The combatants, who had been stripped to the waist, denied that they were fighting for money but had simply fallen out "in the pit".

North Derbyshire continued to hold regular sporting and athletic events. They were always well-supported and included a great variety of disciplines.

Meanwhile in France, Baron Pierre de Coubertain had seen his country invaded by their Prussian neighbours and had become convinced in the value, to a nation, of physical fitness and competition. In 1896 he succeeded in his ambition to stage the first Olympic Games in the modern era.

CHAPTER ELEVEN
The Ragman Comes…

One Saturday in August 1881 six-year-old Eleanor Windle was to meet Alfred Gough, the "Ragman". Their encounter was to lead to tragedy and death – for both of them.

Gough had, briefly, been a police office and served in the army in India. His wife had died whilst he was serving overseas and he had fallen on hard times since returning to civilian life. He was known to indulge in heavy bouts of drinking, often followed by a week or two of sobriety and hard work. His favourite songs were "The Death of Nelson" and, rather ironically, "The Gypsy's Warning".

Gough had been discharged from the army reserve in January 1881 at the age of thirty-four. He made his living by trundling a hand-cart thorough Derbyshire lanes selling children's toys and collecting "rag and bone".

Gough had a "very unprepossessing" appearance. He was described as being greatly pock-marked with a scanty beard and a sandy moustache. He was just under 6 feet tall

Gough had been involved in an incident the day before he encountered Eleanor. On Friday evening, 20 August 1881, he had been seen enticing three young girls to accompany him to Brampton with his hand-cart. This journey was some distance from their homes.

Fortunately, a young lady called Hope Woodward saw Gough take off with Annie Goodwin, Annie Todd and Ada Todd. Hope ran to inform the parents of the girls and John Goodwin, seven-year-old Annie's elder brother was soon in pursuit. He was accompanied by his his brother Frank and a young woman by the name of Harriet Broomhead.

John Goodwin located Gough's hand-cart, complete with the three girls, outside the Grouse Inn in Brampton. Gough had left the children "in charge" whilst he went in for a glass of beer.

Gough re-emerged and was confronted by Goodwin who threatened

The Grouse Inn.

to give him " a good warming".

Later that evening, Mrs Todd sought out Gough and berated him for taking the children off with him. Rather prophetically she said " You will surely get into trouble with this love for children if you take them away from home !"

Mrs Todd went on to tell Gough that she would have reported his conduct to the police had not John Goodwin and his helpers managed to return the girls when they did. Gough replied that "even six" policemen would cause him little anxiety because he had meant no harm and done no wrong.

In the past, though, Gough had fallen foul of the police. He had been under investigation of misconduct towards female servants whilst he was employed as a "bath man" in a Harrogate spa. Police had later found him, the worse for drink, loitering outside the building where the girls were staying.

Gough was arrested and put in the "lock-up". He avoided further punishment because the manager of the spa dropped any charges against Gough on condition that he kept away from the premises.

So the "ragman" that chatted to the little girls in Brimington on Saturday 21 August had a worrying past. However, to young Eleanor and her friends he was just a familiar face who sold the cheap paper flags and toys. Eleanor thought that she might be able to collect a "half-penny" from her mother and she went off with Gough.

The pair were seen by Harriet Johnson, a local schoolmistress. She thought that Gough was behaving inappropriately with the young girl and dashed to arm herself with a broom handle!

Sadly, Gough and Eleanor were a little too far away and Mrs Johnson gave up her pursuit.This was to be the last time that Eleanor was seen alive.

Gough was seen a little later trundling his hand-cart through Brimington and was asked about Eleanor's whereabouts by her father. Gough informed him that he had seen a child answering her description a little down the road near Brimington Cemetery.

Gough then continued to Chesterfield. On his way he met a man known as "Mansfield Tom" who was travelling in the opposite direction. "Mansfield Tom" was clear in his recollection of what Gough said to him – " We have passed one another along this road many a time, but this is the last time we shall do; I have done wrong, and I shall never be happy anymore."

The search for Eleanor became more intense and frantic as the hours passed. It was nearly noon on the following Sunday when Mr.Brown, a local toll-gate keeper, noticed some wheel marks on an unmade road between Staveley and Barrow Hill. There, in a plantation, he discovered Eleanor Windle's body. She had been strangled – the piece of sack cloth still wound around her neck. Nearby was a piece of coloured paper, the sort used in making cheap coloured flags sold by Gough.

Superintendent Carline arrested Alfred Gough in the Buck Inn in Chesterfield on Sunday evening. As Carline approached, Gough remained seated, head down, staring into his glass of beer.

Carline asked Gough if he had been in Brimington the previous day – Gough said that he had been there. Carline asked him about Eleanor – Gough denied knowing anything about her disappearance or death. Gough was arrested and charged with murder.

Understandably, the case caught the public imagination. It appeared, from the witnesses and evidence, that Gough had taken Eleanor to a quiet lane. Here she had been "outraged", brutally beaten and strangled.

Gough had then put her body in his hand-cart and covered it with the toys, "rags and bone". He had then taken the poor unfortunate victim back though her own village on the way to disposal in a more remote spot.

Hundreds of people gathered outside Chesterfield's Marsden Street Police Station to see Gough begin his short journey to West Bars for his first hearing. Shouts and jeers greeted the accused's appearance. There were many women in the crowd and they loudly expressed a wish "that he might be let loose amongst them !"

As Gough left West Bars, after being committed for trial, the crowd surged towards his cab. A young boy, John Molloy, found himself trapped between a wheel and a wall. He had to receive medical attention but, thankfully, was not too seriously injured.

Gough continued to plead his innocence throughout his trial. His defence tried hard to pick fault with the quality and strength of the evidence against their client – but to no avail. Gough was sentenced to death.

Like many Victorian felons, Gough turned to religion in the days before his execution at Derby Gaol. A special prayer was offered up on his behalf by fellow prisoners and, on the Sunday prior to his execution, Gough chose the psalms and hymns at the services.

It was reported that Gough's health and appetite had held up well. He was allowed to smoke whilst taking his open air exercise.

The hangman waiting for Gough was William Marwood.

Marwood was an interesting character. Until the age of fifty-four he had been a cobbler by trade but had a morbid fascination with the methods and mechanics of execution. In 1872 he had begged the Governor of Lincoln Prison to be allowed the opportunity to execute William Frederick Harry.

Marwood was keen to utilise his "long drop" method which, he believed, would bring a rapid death by strangulation. His success had led to a famous career in which he accounted for one hundred and seventy six felons, including eight women. It was Marwood who hanged Kate Webster, the first female to suffer such a fate at Wandsworth Prison.

Marwood also hanged Charles Peace, the famous Victorian burglar and murderer. In 1883, shortly before his death, he was entrusted with executing the four men responsible for the assassination of Lord Frederick Cavendish and Thomas Henry Burke in Phoenix Park, Dublin.

The man waiting for Alfred Gough was already so famous that he featured in popular songs and rhymes. Marwood was one of the two original hangman immortalised in the "Punch and Judy" puppet show.

At ten minutes to eight on Monday morning at thousand people had gathered outside the wall where the scaffold was situated. The scaffold was a stark structure – just three iron bars with a stout rope hanging from the horizontal bar.

Close to the scaffold was the "pinioning place". Gough entered this space wearing a faded green coat and a pair of corduroy trousers that had frequently been darned and mended.

Gough was quite composed, although he appeared a little pale. He had not slept well.

The Chaplain began to recite the opening sentence of the Burial Service whilst, simultaneously, Marwood secured Gough's arms to his body. Gough remained steady throughout and declined to make use of the stool that had been provided for him.

After a quick gulp of some water from a flask handed to him by the warders, Gough walked towards the scaffold. He stood there, looking up to the heavens. Marwood swiftly, but carefully, adjusted the rope around Gough's neck and placed the white hood over his face.

The Chaplain recited a prayer and, as he reached the verse – "Man that is born of a woman hath but a short time to live" – Marwood slid the bolt. Gough disappeared from view.

The was a brief pause. The doctor drew aside the cloth and looked down at the prisoner. Death had been instantaneous.

Gough's body was left to hang for an hour whilst the usual legal formalities were signed and posted outside the gates of the prison. The Chaplain also circulated copies of a letter written by Alfred Gough just prior to his execution:

"HM Prison Derby November 21st 1881

Sir (to the Minister)

I now take my pen in my hand to write a few lines to thank you for being so good and kind to me, poor unfortunate prisoner, who committed such a fearful, wicked crime. I hope the Lord will forgive me for it. I am very sorry for it; if I had a hundred lives I would give them to call that poor, sweet, innocent little girl back to life; but it cannot be. But the Lord has taken her soul to Heaven to be with the angels of glory, in that bright and happy land above, where there is no sorrow, but all is bliss and happiness; to which I hope my Lord and Saviour will lift me up, and wash all my wicked sin away and make me as white as snow, and to sing the praises of Jesus Christ our Lord and Saviour for ever and ever, amen.

Goodbye and God bless you sir, for being so kind to me, a poor sinner. I shall be cold and in the dust, but hope to be forgiven and rise in glory at the last day.

So no more, yours truly

Alfred Gough.

May God bless you, and the doctor for his kindness and likewise the Governor."

Gough clearly wanted this particular letter to be made public. He had previously written a confession for his brother-in-law and asked the Governor to destroy it. He had discovered that members of his family had been selling his correspondence to newspapers in Sheffield.

This sad case was to trouble the local courts a little further. George Wragg, a labourer from Sheffield Road in Chesterfield found himself up before the Magistrates. He had been part of a gang of "roughs" who had targeted the schoolmistress Harriett Johnson – the witness to the abduction of Eleanor Windle.

There was a feeling in some quarters that Johnson's actions had not been sufficiently robust at that crucial time. A large group of young men had gathered outside the home of the Johnsons – taking advantage of the fact that a constable who was providing protection had temp-orarily left for "refreshments".

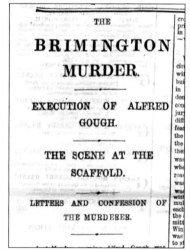

Threats were made and a few men then went around the rear of the property to steal apples from the orchard. P.C. Wright returned and apprehended Wragg. The constable was assisted by a member of the public, Thomas Martin. The latter was to lose a portion of his finger as Wragg bit him.

Gough's case merits a full page supplement in the Derbyshire Times, *26 November 1881*

CHAPTER TWELVE
Too Late for Temperance

Nowadays, the Vicar Lane area of Chesterfield is a modern, spacious shopping precinct. In 1888, it was somewhat different.

"Barracks Yard " had formerly been the home of the Derbyshire Militia and was known locally as the "Dark Hole". The name was descriptive. It was a desperate place for Arthur and Alice Delaney to live.

Arthur was thirty-one years of age and Alice was four years younger. They had married in 1884 and had two young children, the eldest three years old and the youngest just three months. In April 1888 Alice was pregnant with the couple's third child. The Delaney household, though, was not a happy one.

Arthur and Alice had separated on more than one occasion. In February 1887, Arthur had appeared before the Borough Magistrates charged with an aggravated assault on his wife. He had been fined 10s and was given a separation and maintenance order.

Neighbours firmly believed that Delaney, an engine fitter by trade, had never forgiven his wife for making their "difficulties" public. Despite this, and Arthur's further convictions for drunkenness and wilful damage, Alice moved back in with him. She continued to complain about his conduct towards her.

On 21 April 1888, Arthur and Alice Delaney went the short distance around the corner from their home to the "Red Lion" public house. Frederick Keeton, the landlord, remembered very clearly their arrival at round 2.30 in the afternoon.

The Delaneys sat together in the back parlour. Arthur was drinking rum and Alice was partaking of sherry. According to Keeton, though, they were both perfectly sober. They fell out, though, when Mrs McHugh, a neighbour turned up.

Mrs McHugh had called in to the Red Lion to purchase a quart of beer to take home for her husband. Alice had gone across to speak to her and ask her to have a drink. Arthur Delaney was angry at this and was heard to say "I'll kill you before the night's over !" when Alice returned. Alice, for her part, replied "Ah, that is more than you dare do !"

Frederick Keeton did not believe that Alice was afraid and just took the words as idle threats. He did, though, ask the pair to leave his premises.

However, at midnight, Keeton was disturbed in his kitchen by the sounds of a woman screaming. He went out at once and was immediately joined by two of the Delaney's neighbours – Thomas McHugh and Thomas Spooner.

They were soon at the door of the Delaney's house, the screams seemed be coming from inside. The door was locked and bolted but the men were able to burst it open.

Once inside, they saw Alice Delaney laying on the floor with the baby in her arms. Her head had been "battered in".

Arthur Delaney was standing, quietly, holding a poker in his hand. It was covered in blood.

He made no attempt to escape as Keeton grabbed him by the collar and took him to the Police Station. When asked why he had done what he had – Delaney replied very calmly that he would "answer that question at the proper time". He appeared sober and collected.

Thomas Spooner, an ironmonger's assistant lived two doors away. He had heard what he believed to be the sound of sticks being chopped accompanied by the call of "murder" several times. He remembered hearing at least "nine or ten" blows.

Thomas McHugh, likewise, had been alerted by the cries for help and the sound of blows.

Alice Delaney, who was between three and four months pregnant, was still alive as she was taken to Chesterfield Hospital. She had received severe injuries to her head and face. Her left cheek bone was fractured and her left eye was "in a sorry state".

Alice also had multiple cuts to her scalp and the middle finger of her left hand was broken. The tip of that finger was missing. Her arms were badly bruised but she was still conscious and able to dictate a statement:

"I am the wife of Arthur Thomas Delaney of Barracks Yard, Chesterfield. I reached home directly after eleven o'clock on Saturday night and my husband and children were there. No one else was present. We did not go to bed. He gave me a shilling to get something for his supper and I went out. The shops were closed. When I got back

I told him I could not get anything for him. He wanted to lock the door. He struck me many times with a poker. All the injuries, the marks which are on my person were caused by him striking me with the poker. I cried out when he struck me. He continued to strike me with the poker until someone came. My two little children were present. The eldest is three and a half years old. In consequence of the injuries I have received I think my life is in danger."

Alice Delaney bravely fought for her life for many weeks, the damage to her brain was followed by blood poisoning. She finally died on 12 July 1888.

At his trial for murder, Arthur Delaney's defence was based upon a claim of insanity. This was, apparently, triggered by Alice's return to the family home on that fateful April night.

Mr. Hextall, defending, cited the fact that Delaney's father had committed suicide in 1879 whilst an inmate at the County Lunatic Asylum at Mickleover. This line of defence was further supported by the fact that Arthur's aunt, Ann Delaney, had died in the same asylum a matter of weeks before the attack on Alice.

Entrance to Vicar Lane.

The jury also heard that Delaney had been made aware by his wife of possible "intimacy with another man". He had said, on being interviewed by Police the morning after the attack :

"All I can say is, when she came home last night she said she had been with another man, and if that is not enough to make a fellow turn round – I don't know what is."

The jury retired for eleven minutes only. Arthur Thomas Delaney was found guilty of wilful murder. When asked if he had anything to say before sentence was passed, Delaney, belatedly, showed some thought for his wife –

"I should wish to say that the expressions I have used against my wife about her being with other men are all untrue. Now that she is dead I wish to say in respect to her memory that it is not true."

Arthur Delaney was then sentenced to death. The judge made it clear that, even if he could have reprieved him, he would not have done so, saying –

"In all my experience I have rarely met with more brutal violence towards one whom a man is bound to shelter and protect, brutal violence terminating in death under more sickening and painful circumstances. Your days are numbered."

Delaney had spent most of his trial avidly following every word and movement of counsel but seemed oblivious to any other feature of his surroundings. The judge had barely finished his sentencing as Delaney suddenly turned around and made for the cells. He tripped as he reached the top of the steps and made a most unceremonious exit.

Delaney was taken to Derby Gaol where he was placed in the Condemned Cell.

Normal practice dictated that an execution would take place on the first Monday after three Sundays had elapsed since sentencing. However, a change in routine meant that the execution would have to take place much later in the week. This proved convenient because Mr Berry, the hangman, had a prior "engagement" in Manchester on Tuesday. Delaney's execution was scheduled for Friday.

James Berry of Bradford was a very experienced executioner. A "fresh complexioned, pleasant featured man", he had already despatched 126 felons. On occasion, he was capable of exhibiting a shred of sympathy with some of those who came his way. However, Berry had made it very clear that he regarded Delaney as a particularly "loathsome" individual.

The scaffold to be used was the same one that had been erected for the execution of Alfred Gough a few years previously. It was in the "outer portal " of Derby Gaol. The location had other grim features for Delaney. The scaffold was flanked by the nine graves of recently processed criminals.

The view of the scaffold from neighbouring properties had been screened by the erection of wooden covers. Effectively, the scaffold with its noose and trapdoor was situated in a shed construction.

The restricted view did not discourage a large crowd on the day of the execution. At half past six on Friday morning people began to arrive and gather close to the wall where the scaffold was situated. Just before the appointed time at a quarter to eight the crowd numbered in excess of two thousand. Some had walked all the way from Chesterfield to witness the raising of the black flag.

Mr Berry had arrived on Thursday. He had inspected the noose, which was already in place from an execution two days previously. He found it to be strongly made of hemp and approaching three quarters of an inch in thickness.

Berry had also done his calculations for the "drop". Delaney weighed just a little over 10 stones but Berry had allowed for a weight of up to 13 stones to ensure there would be no mishap.

Berry would have been very careful in his planning. Three years previously he had been the executioner who failed, on three attempts, to execute John Babbacombe Lee in Exeter. The Home Secretary had been forced to commute Lee's sentence to life imprisonment after the gallows trapdoor failed to operate.

Berry spent Thursday night within the confines of the prison. Nearby, Delaney was staring out of his cell window until it went dark and he could see no more. He then ate his supper and went to bed.

Delaney awoke early on Friday morning. He washed, ate some bread and butter and drank tea. He was then visited by Rev. Crellin, the Chaplain, who helped him with prayers. Delaney continued to pray in his cell until just a few minutes before eight o'clock.

Berry would normally shake hands with the condemned prisoner and then tie some restraints whilst in the cell. His disapproval of the crime that Delaney had committed meant that Berry merely restrained the prisoners arms whilst they were outside in the corridor. No handshake took place.

Delaney did not need any support from the two wardens at either side of him as he made his way to the scaffold. He was wearing the same clothes that he had worn at his trial. His clothes, though, had been brushed and his shoes were clean.

He noticed the large number of reporters waiting for him but he quickly looked down at the ground as he passed. Delaney did not appear to notice the freshly dug grave that had been prepared for him.

Delaney stood on the trapdoor as Berry placed the white hood over his head and the noose around his neck. He spoke his final words " Lord, into thy hand I commend my spirit. May the Lord have mercy on my soul. Lord Jesus receive my spirit."

His voice held firm until the very last when he began to tremble a little.

As the last word was uttered Berry quickly withdrew the bolt on the trapdoor.

Delaney fell with a thud into the pit below. The events on the scaffold had played out for less than thirty seconds. Berry believed that a murderer such as Delaney denied his victim mercy and time – and he deserved no better.

The Doctors present looked down at Delaney for nearly ten minutes before deciding that he was clearly dead. Dr Greaves reported later that all movement had actually ceased after seven minutes.

By eleven o'clock, Arthur Thomas Delaney had been buried in a plain wooden coffin "wholly devoid of all fittings, furniture or ornament". Quicklime was placed in the coffin to assist decomposition.

Delaney's story has a footnote in the form of a letter written in prison and delivered after his death.

He was addressing the "Lifeboat Lodge of Good Templars", a temperance society in Brampton, Chesterfield –

"My dear friends

I write you farewell on this earth but hope with God's great mercy to meet you all there were there will be no more sorrow or temptation.

I do sincerely thank you for your kindness to me and hope that my fall will be the means of, with God's help, lifting others up from a drunkards grave.

Had I followed your advice my poor wife would have been

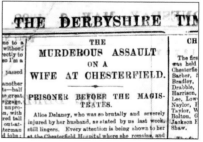

Arthur Delaney – 2nd May, 1888, the Derbyshire Times

alive now and we should have been happy for she was a faithful and good wife to me. God knows that I should not have done such a dreadful crime. If I had kept my pledge, but hope it will be a warning to those that play with the devil in soulution.

Will you tell …to give is heart to God and he will be safe from is great curse the drink bid him and is wife farewell for me and tell him to put all is power to work to help the noble work of Temperance onward for it is God's work – oh do implore that that is playing with the drink to abstain from it for it is a national curse.

Now farewell, to you all and may God prosper your noble work.

From your unfortunate friend.

Arthur T. Delaney"

CHAPTER THIRTEEN
Suffer Little Children…Again

In 1889 a collier from Swanwick was to provide a grim link between Mary Whitfield, Arthur Delaney and James Berry.

George Horton was a widower who lived with his seven children. His daughter Kate shared her room with her younger brother Joseph in the overcrowded family home. The Bowskill family also lived in the house.

George had taken out an insurance policy on Kate on 23 April 1889 which would pay out £7 in the event of her death. In May Kate was in good health as she returned from chapel to the family home.

Later on Kate began to feel ill and complained of a pain in her stomach. She was still unwell as she retired to bed.

Early next morning Kate awoke with a raging thirst and asked for a drink. George Horton said that he did not have the time to bring her one because he needed to go the colliery to start his shift. He left the house. Kate went to wake her elder sister, Sarah Jane.

It was clear to Sarah Jane that there was something seriously wrong. Kate was not only desperately thirsty but her eyes and mouth appeared to be twitching in an uncontrolled manner. She was also becoming quite stiff.

Sarah Jane picked Kate up and shouted for help, alerting Mrs Bowskill. Mrs Evans, a neighbour, heard the commotion and arrived on the scene and gave Kate water which she gratefully gulped.

Sadly, Kate's condition rapidly worsened. She was dead before a doctor arrived.

At half past eight George Horton returned home unexpectedly. He was told what had happened to Kate and then confronted by Mrs Brown and Mrs Bowskill who were suspicious about the death of his daughter.

Whilst Kate had been rapidly deteriorating she had been questioned by her neighbours who were seeking any possible cause of her condition. Kate had said that she had been given "some blue stuff out of a bottle with a white cap" to drink by her father.

Horton angrily dismissed any thought that he would harm his own child. He became very emotional and kissed Kate – his tear drops falling on to the unfortunate child's cheek.

He soon recovered sufficient composure to strike his son George in the face. George had been heard to tell some local boys that Kate was dead and that she had been given "some blue stuff out of a bottle" by their father.

Indeed, when Kate's body was eventually examined some small "bluish" particles were found to be present in her system. Strychnine poisoning was identified as the cause of her death.

George Horton was put on trial for the murder of his daughter.

His defence argued that there was no proof that he had any poison in his possession or that he had actually administered it. It was entirely possible, they argued, that if there was any poison in the home, Kate could have mistakenly taken it herself after her father left for work.

The jury, though, believed that Horton had murdered Kate to secure the £7 insurance pay out. He was found guilty and sentenced to death.

Horton did not accept the verdict and proclaimed " I am innocent" as he was escorted from the court.

A fortnight's confinement in Derby Gaol seemed to have an effect on Horton's conscience. Rev. Matthews, the vicar of Swanwick, visited Horton in his cell and asked him directly if he had murdered Kate. "Yes I did it" was Horton's reply.

Horton went on to tell Rev. Matthews that he had procured the poison shortly before Kate's death. He had been forced into such a drastic plan of action because he found himself in the direst of financial straights. He feared that he would lose his home and the family would be broken up. The insurance money was to be his salvation.

He gave Kate the poison and hoped that she would die peacefully in her sleep. When he left home that morning he did not go to work, but wandered in the fields for a while. He took the opportunity to dispose of the bottle that had contained the strychnine.

Once he had managed to confess, Horton's demeanour changed. Previously he had appreared very callous and indifferent but now he began to spend more and more time with Rev. Matthews and Rev. Crellin, the Prison Chaplain.

Prior to his arrest Horton had shown little affection any of his children. He had already managed to send two away and publicly had been heard to remark "I have got shut of two children and very soon I will be shut of

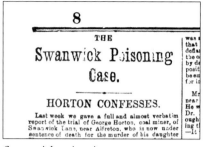

8

THE

Swanwick Poisoning
Case.

HORTON CONFESSES.

Last week we gave a full and almost verbatim report of the trial of George Horton, coal miner, of Swanwick Lane, near Alfreton, who is now under sentence of death for the murder of his daughter

Swanwick poisoning case,
8 June 1889, Derbyshire Times.

the rest."

However, Horton now wrote to the Guardian of the Belper Workhouse and begged to be given the opportunity to meet his family. The Guardian agreed and a very emotional meeting took place. The bedraggled youngsters appeared in their workhouse clothes. They were repeatedly kissed by their tearful father as the supervising warders looked on.

In Derby Gaol, Horton occupied the same cell as Arthur T. Delaney. He enjoyed a "first-class" prison diet. In the days before his execution he suffered from a severe bout of diarrhoea – this was attributed to nervousness rather than poor food. He was allowed a quarter ounce of tobacco a day but no alcohol.

Horton was to be executed by James Berry who, of course, had been responsible for dealing with Delaney. The scaffold, though, was a different one. Its original iron beam had been replaced with a wooden one. Berry had decided that such a refinement would result in less "spring" when the body fell.

Berry had tested the rope and a "drop" of six feet had been allowed for instead of the five feet six inches originally planned. Berry made this re-adjustment because, although Horton was only five feet three inches tall, he was powerfully built and possessed a "strong muscular neck".

Horton was calm prior to the day of his execution. He spent his time in prayer and writing a number of letters to his friends and family.

Horton slept so well the night before that he had to be roused by a warder at six o'clock. He dressed himself and went for a stroll around the prison courtyard for about half an hour in the company of a warder.

Horton returned to the cell and ate the self-same breakfast as that "enjoyed" by Delaney – bread, butter and tea. Again, as Delaney had been, he was joined for prayers by the Rev. Crellin.

At 7.53a.m. the Chief Warder, Macauley, entered the cell and Horton began to prepare in earnest for his execution. Soon a small procession of Horton, warders, officials, the Chaplain and police surgeons made its way into the prison yard.

Berry met Horton and "pinioned" very efficiently. As Berry was securing Horton's arms the latter murmured "Oh Lord, receive my soul".

Horton then walked on. Head bowed.

He passed the line of graves and, like Delaney, seemed to ignore his own resting place – already dug and covered, for the moment, with a board.

Horton continued to pray until he found himself actually positioned on top of the trapdoor. Berry quickly placed the white hood over Horton's head and without hesitation slid the bolt. Horton's, perhaps rather surprised by Berry's efficiency shouted simply – "Oh!"

This time the proceedings on the actual scaffold had only accounted for twenty seconds.

The surgeons and warders at first looked down at Horton in the pit below but soon climbed down the ladder to examine the body more closely.

Just before Berry slid the bolt Horton had clasped his hands in an attitude of prayer. His fingers remained in the same position after death.

Delaney had taken seven minutes to finally be still as the result of strangulation. Horton, given a "longer drop" by Berry had died almost instantaneously.

Shortly afterwards, in 1891, Berry was to become the first executioner to resign. The employment was well paid at £10 per death warrant – he was earning between £250 and £350 per annum.

After more than 130 executions Berry decided to go to America and attempt a series of lecture tours. He was not terribly successful but claimed to his dying day that he had executed the real "Jack the Ripper" – a felon by the name of William Bury.

CHAPTER FOURTEEN
A Champion Jockey and Church Bells

Northumberland Derbyshire would not readily spring to mind if you were studying the history of horse-racing. However, a visit to Newmarket the birthplace of the "sport of kings", would reveal a clue that Chesterfield made a significant contribution.

Fred Archer, the greatest jockey of the nineteenth century, is buried at Newmarket. Archer was a national sporting icon. The "Tinman", as he was known, rode 2748 winners and headed the list of jockeys from 1873 until he committed suicide aged just twenty-nine in 1886. His funeral was a grand affair attended by members of the landed gentry. Amongst the many floral tributes was one from the Prince of Wales.

Fred Archer's impressive memorial at Newmarket has an inscription which records his first victory on 28 September 1870. He had ridden "Athol Daisy" in the Nursery Handicap at Chesterfield Races. His weight was recorded as 6st 5lb and he was thirteen years old.

The young Fred Archer was riding at a well-established meeting in 1870 at Chesterfield. It was in 1727 that horse-racing had first taken place on the two mile track in Whittington Moor, making it the second oldest meeting in the country. At the first meeting, the Earl of Scarsdale donated a plate to the value of £40 for the winner in a four horse race. It was won by "Tory" owned by a Mr Beighton.

Meetings were held annually under Newmarket rules and attracted large crowds. In 1829, the Duke of Devonshire, a keen patron, was instrumental in encouraging the addition of a grandstand on the course.

The grandstand was similar in style to that at Doncaster but sadly the building costs proved more than the Duke and local investors had contributed. An ingenious "silver ticket" scheme was set up. In this, anyone who contributed a minimum of £5 received a token guaranteeing

Fred Archer – the Tinman.

them "free" entry for life.

The investment in the grand-stand was clearly more successful socially than financially. In 1837 the start of the meeting was signalled by the arrival of the Duke of Devonshire's state carriage, accompanied by eight outriders. The Duke himself did not attend until later as he was assisting the Earl of Burlington who had, ironically, fallen from his horse. The party, though, did include the Hon. G. H. and Lady Louisa Cavendish and a number of their titled friends.

The Cavendish party joined the "Stand" which was "well-filled with the beauty and fashion of the neighbourhood".

In the evening there was a meal and ball at the Angel Inn. The meal was described as being excellent with the wines of "first quality" and a dessert having "every description of hot-house and other fruits."

The entertainment provided was not restricted to the aristocratic and well-heeled. Local inns competed to procure the best "booth " locations. In 1860 Samuel Gregory of the Red Lion Brampton was able to boast in the local newspaper that he had "taken the Grand Stand" and, as usual, the booth opposite.

Thomas Lenthall of the Vine Tavern Sheffield compensated for only having "Booth No.3" by promising "Ales and Spirits of first-rate quality "

Competition for punters was truly intense. John Dutton of The Old Spinning Wheel, Glumangate offered "all kinds of refreshments of good quality and at reasonable prices". He also offered customers the opportunity to use his rifle practice room with "a first-class selection of rifles always in readiness" !

Charles Whittaker of the Red Lion, Vicar Lane offered in the evening of each race day "a Quadrille Band". William Hanstock of the Castle Inn countered by providing a company of "Gleesingers" throughout the day in booths 18 and 19.

Chesterfield Races clearly provided great entertainment for all. Sideshows tempted people to knock down wooden dolls with a variety of missiles. Others offered the opportunity to kick footballs through holes in canvas sheets. There were exhibitions of the "noble art of self-defence", fire eaters and the like. In 1887 there was, in honour of Queen Victoria, the opportunity for a lavish "Jubilee Sweepstake".

"Touts" were everywhere promising to name the winning horse for "threepence or sixpence". A considerable appetite for betting and rather boisterous behaviour seemed to permeate all classes of society and not just the "influx of persons of low habits and depraved character". This situation caused a dilemma for the religious community in Chesterfield.

At first the church bells of St Mary's had been rung to signify the beginning of race days and draw people to the event. This was not a spontaneous action – the Race Committee had astutely arranged to pay the bell-ringers £2 per year for their trouble.

However, by 1849 Archdeacon Thomas Hill was sufficiently concerned to advise decent folk to say away "from a scene so perilous to their bodily safety and their spiritual welfare." He also banned the ringing of the church bells on race days. Thomas Hill only managed to do this by agreeing to continue to pay the bell-ringers the £2 out of his own pocket to maintain the dignified silence!

Despite the disapproval of Archdeacon Hill, Chesterfield Races continued to grow and offer popular leisure activities despite having to re-establish itself after 1877, when the Race Committee could no longer guarantee the required prize fund. The event carried on under less stringent regulations.

In the late 1890s, "Proctors Bioscope " was a regular feature of the trackside entertainment. This was an early example of cinematographic technology – "singing pictures". Well-attended and eagerly awaited, the shows were accompanied by a massive Gavioli organ and a troupe of dancing girls.

Such a gathering was always likely to attract punters of dubious character. In 1902 a Police Officer observed a man place his hand in a lady's pocket. When searched he had "a gentleman's gold watch, a lady's trinket chain, a gold ring and two pawn tickets sewn into his trouser bottoms." Such incidents were becoming all too frequent.

The twentieth-century saw a decline in the standard of horse-racing as well as the behaviour of some race-goers. In 1923 the *Derby Evening Telegraph* said that Chesterfield Races had "degenerated into what was known in racing circles as a flapping meeting."

Chesterfield was expanding and land for building houses was badly needed, the race meeting had become, for many, a public nuisance. The course now crossed several roads. Stories were told of jockeys calling into public houses during races. Even worse were allegations that jockeys sometimes mixed up their horses during such breaks and finished on different mounts.

Eventually, Chesterfield Town Council decided to put a bill before Parliament to remove the right to hold horse-racing on Whittington Moor. The Race Committee was compensated to the tune of £250.

The last meeting took place on 29 July 1924. It was a rather chaotic affair for an event that had, in its heyday, attracted 50,000 spectators. There were not enough jockeys and George Smith, a former groom to the Royal Horse Artillery offered to help out. He won the final three races held at the course.

The Crooked Spire – its bells were sometimes deemed inappropriate for horse racing.

CHAPTER FIFTEEN
Now You See Her…

The tiny and tranquil village of Smalldale near Bradwell was the focus of much attention in the summer of 1885. A violent marriage, allegations of incest, a suicide and the disappearance of a wife were ingredients of an enduring mystery.

The events, as they unfolded, were to involve an isolated cowshed, a lime kiln, a freshly dug vegetable patch and a recently walled-in bedroom chimney.

Smalldale – this charming community was the scene of the Bradwell Mystery.

The focus of attention was to be Matthew James Buttery – known locally as just "James". He was forty-seven years old and a strong, powerfully-built man. He was the husband of Martha who was thirteen years older. Once she was described as being "comely" but, by 1885, was of a very slight build and "worn almost to a shadow."

The Butterys were not rich but they were quite comfortably off – the property and money being derived from Martha's side of the family. They had three daughters but they had all left home – one was local in Alrewas, the other two had moved to Brighton and Manchester respectively.

James Buttery had a reputation for being a hard drinker and often being violent towards his wife. Martha was known to frequently absent herself when things took a turn for the worse. She often left home for two or three days to allow things to calm down. Martha often stayed with her sister who lived nearby. When she did return home she would often defend her husband against any allegations of wrongdoing.

Hence, it was not until about two weeks had passed without a sighting of Martha that people in the village began to be concerned. She was clearly not staying with her sister and rumours of foul play began to circulate as things had been particularly volatile between the Butterys of late.

James, for his part, was going about his business perfectly normally. He had been seen looking after his cattle, doing routine repairs and strolling around the village as usual.

However, the police were alerted by concerned locals and Sergeant Gray from Castleton went to see James Buttery to make enquiries. James received them without any hint of guilt and actively assisted them in their enquiries from the beginning. He insisted that there was no need for alarm. He repeated, no doubt, what the police had already been told – Martha often disappeared but always returned.

James Buttery made a full statement to Sergeant Gray. His wife had gone to bed at 9 o'clock on Thursday night, April 30th. He had awoken at five o'clock the following morning and Martha was nowhere to be seen. The door that he had locked and bolted the previous evening was now open.

Buttery admitted that they had fallen out and that Martha had threatened to go and stay with their daughter in Alrewas. He assumed that she had done this.

Buttery went on to say that a sum of money – more than £300 – was missing from the house and he thought that Martha would have taken this with her. He then shocked the police by saying that the cause of their most recent argument was the fact that James had accused Martha of infidelity with Joseph Wright. Joseph was Martha's brother.

This allegation, when it became public knowledge, caused outrage in the village. Martha Buttery may have had a rather hot temper herself but was generally regarded as having led "a blameless life".

James Buttery found it unbearable being the object of so much gossip and suspicion. He went to the local Vicarage to see the Rev. H.T. Dudley and said that he felt unfairly accused. He was advised to put all his energy into searching for his wife as this would solve most of his problems.

Buttery next went to see his sister who kept the Bowling Green Tavern in Smalldale. Nancy asked him straight – "Now, Jim, hast thou made away with her? You know its bound to come out, now they have begun to search, they will find her dead or alive. I want you to tell the truth." Buttery answered unambiguously and without hesitation – " I know nothing about her, I have not seen her since she went out of the house."

Buttery went on to tell Nancy that he intended asking one of his daughters to return home and "keep house". He felt that he could not stand the situation much longer.

James Buttery returned home. He was never seen alive again.

Buttery's body was discovered by the police – he had hanged himself with a rope fastened to the corner of a doorframe.

James Buttery's suicide may have denied the investigation into Martha's disappearance its key witness but it did little to slow the pace of enquiries.

Buttery's sister kept the Bowling Green Tavern in Smalldale.

The inquest into Buttery's death was held at the same Bowling Green Tavern where James may have had his last conversation. Naturally the questioning strayed into issues that could shine some light on Martha's fate or whereabouts.

William Buttery, James' brother, gave evidence. He was able to confirm that James had been consistent in his account of Martha's disappearance. He had been told exactly the same details as James had told the police as the two were chatting together at Hope Fair.

William did notice that James appeared a bit "low" and said that, in his opinion, his brother had "not been right for years – ever since he had sustained an accident and a cart ran over his head!" According to William, James believed that he was influenced by the moon.

It became clear that the local police had some inkling that Buttery thought his wife was being unfaithful. On one occasion Martha had been seen sporting a black eye. This was shortly after Buttery had been heard talking about her infidelity.

The police had been searching old lead mining shafts which were everywhere in the locality. They had also dragged meres and placed advertisements in all local newspapers.

Local people began to talk of a "fearful smell" emanating from the Buttery's house. This fuelled the story that Martha had been "walled-up" in the recently replastered bedroom chimney.

The fact that Buttery, just before his death, had been observed digging the ground intending to plant turnips provided another focus of attention. The land was extensively poked with iron spikes – to no avail.

The Buttery's garden contained an old well. There, people speculated, Buttery could have disposed of Martha's body. This theory was discredited following thorough investigation using a "grave digger's rod".

A much more promising location was a cowshed some distance from the house. A pair of boots belonging to Martha were found there. Four cartloads of manure were removed and carefully examined – but nothing was found.

The floor of the cowshed was dug up but revealed no secrets. However, a nearby limekiln was strongly favoured by locals as the most likely place to dispose of a body.

Joseph Wright, Martha's brother, was not interviewed immediately. It was felt that the charges made by Buttery were so outrageous that they were not "worthy of credence".

Some of the villagers believed Buttery to be innocent. It was entirely possible, they said, that Martha could have left the area and set herself up with the sum of money she was supposedly carrying. It was also possible that she could have accidently fallen down one of the dangerous mine shafts.

The police, in the absence of a body, did not discount such theories. A local blacksmith was asked to make special extra long probes for use in some flooded mine shafts. A mastiff and a St Bernard dog were also enlisted.

Most locals, though, were adamant. Martha had been murdered. They believed it impossible for a woman to wander around in the early morning in a farming community without being spotted by someone.

In February 1886, a chance conversation in a Buxton public house was reported in a newspaper. A man claiming to be from Smalldale said that he had seen Martha, alive and well, in Sheffield.

People in Smalldale and Bradwell claimed never to have heard of the man who made the "sighting". The mystery continued.

Tiny Smalldale makes the headlines –
Derbyshire Times *6 June 1885.*

CHAPTER SIXTEEN
Brampton – All Lit Up!

In 1863, Britain found itself gripped in the fervour that surrounded the celebration the marriage of the Prince of Wales to Princess Alexandra of Denmark.

Locally, special events would take place in Walton, Staveley, Eckington, New Whittington and on "Derby Lane". Brampton, though, found itself in the enviable position of being able to hold a lavish double celebration.

One hundred and fifty years ago industrial development in North Derbyshire was moving on at a rapid pace. Brampton was no exception and was experiencing significant growth. Change and modernisation were necessary.

In January of 1863 a packed, and rather heated, meeting had taken the decision to allow the Chesterfield Gas Company to erect and light thirty gas lamps in lower Brampton. Each lamp was to cost 50 shillings a year to operate – the same as those already in use in Chesterfield itself.

The decision was far from unanimous – a number of local residents objected to the inevitable increase in rates because they would not actually be lit up!

The Gas Company expected to be able to complete the entire project within six weeks. The big ceremonial inaugural lighting could, therefore, be engineered to coincide with the national celebrations of the forthcoming Royal Wedding.

The Chesterfield Gas Company was true to its word and the work had been completed two weeks ahead of schedule. Brampton was ready to publicly display its growing prosperity.

At eleven o'clock on the day of the wedding a large procession began to form on "Mr Briddon's Field". The Briddon family were the owners of the Barker Pottery. At the time, there were eight thriving "earthenware" manufacturers in business just in the area of lower Brampton.

The Cutthorpe Band marched at the head of clergy, businessmen, tradesmen, Sunday School children and inspectors from the Chesterfield Gas Company!

The procession moved through the district of Brampton that was soon to be lit. It snaked along the old road to St Thomas' church and then, by the "new road" to the Wheatbridge Pottery. It then returned to the School Room …via the Gas Works!

At the School Room a hymn and the National Anthem were sung. Afterwards a thousand buns were distributed amongst children present.

The Red Lion Inn then took centre stage as it hosted a public dinner. The "large room" was filled to capacity by representatives of Brampton's burgeoning business community. The Master of Ceremonies was pottery manufacturer Edward Wright who, at the age of eighty-nine, was described as "the venerable father of commerce in Brampton".

Attention to Victorian lighting.

There was a great deal of mutual congratulation and comprehensive toasting –" The manufacturing interests of Brampton", " The Healths of the Directors of the Chesterfield Gas Company" followed, by "The Press" – a clear barometer of the level of good nature!

Finally, the "Health of the Ladies" was proposed by Mr Walton Wright and seconded by Mr Adam Taylor who was deemed to be the youngest bachelor in the room.

Attention later moved outside where eager competitors were attempting to climb a "greasy pole" that had been erected in Mr Briddon's field. A copper tea kettle was perched on the top as the prize for the first successful climber. There were many failures before the prestigious trophy was grabbed by James Ford. The young man gleefully carried off his kettle through cheering crowds!

Throughout the day cannons were fired. On one occasion a cannon burst showering fragments of hot metal in all directions. Luckily, there were no injuries.

The factories, potteries and inns of Brampton were festooned with an array of banners and flags. However, there was still an important phase of the festivities to come.

At dusk, Brampton's streets were lit by the new gas lamps for the first time. As soon as the first lamp was lit, a rocket was fired into the sky. The large crowd roared its approval and the band began to play.

There were gasps of approval as a "pretty illumination" depicting the feathers of the emblem of the Prince of Wales with a star at either side, flickered into life. This impressive montage was fixed to two of the larger gas lamps.

Everyone seemed to agree that the lighting was "brilliant in the extreme" as attention turned again to events on Mr Briddon's field. Here there was a large bonfire which warmed the crowd that had gathered to witness fireworks.

Unsurprisingly, the streets of Brampton remained thronged well into the evening. Local inns responded to the extra demand by offering "dinners at a nominal charge". Dancing continued until late.

The Royal Oak Inn made its bid to be a focal point by suspending an evergreen archway across the road outside. This celebratory feature had a crown and the letters V.R. prominently displayed.

Sadly, everyday life in Brampton one hundred and fifty years ago sometimes had a less joyous side. A few weeks after the festivities, James Lowe and Henry Lowe were charged by the Chesterfield Gas Company with "wilfully extinguishing lamps in Brampton".

The lamps in question had been lit by John Longden, the lamplighter. However, after much consideration of various accounts of men climbing up lamp posts the accused were discharged for lack of evidence.

Soon afterwards Thomas Johnson and Abraham Gascoyne were not as fortunate as they committed the opposite offence. They had been seen to leave the Red Lion public house, climb up and *light* a "public lamp". It burned very brightly but, unfortunately, rather too brightly. In the morning the whole bracket was "burnt down and the glass broken". An expert witness, William Thorpe, confirmed that the light had been improperly lit.

The situation worsened for the accused as it emerged that Thorpe had discovered six lamps burning furiously in the early hours of the morning in question.

The damage to the lamps was estimated at sixteen shillings. Gascoyne was discharged but Johnson was fined one shilling and had to pay for half the damage caused to the lamps. He was given two weeks to pay – failure was to result in a fourteen day prison sentence.

Such antics clearly continued, forcing the Chesterfield Gas Company to offer the considerable sum of £10 as a reward for information concerning such "maliciously disposed person or persons". The tactic was, evidently, successful as six further individuals were soon identified.

The Royal Oak – site of the "evergreen archway".

CHAPTER SEVENTEEN
Kissing Cousins – A Pathway to Murder

John Walker of Middle Handley repaired a stile in 1873. Unwittingly, he provided the materials for a brutal murder.

In April 1873 a badly beaten body was discovered in rural North Derbyshire. It was Elizabeth Hudson – known locally as Eliza. The injuries to her skull and face were so severe that she was virtually unrecognisable.

The murderer was Benjamin Hudson. He was Eliza's husband - but also her cousin. Benjamin was an illegitimate twin son of Mary Hudson. Mary was the sister of Richard Hudson who was the unfortunate Eliza's father.

Benjamin had always been close to Eliza. For years before they were married he had developed an obsessive jealousy on her account. He regularly followed her around and became angry and agitated if he observed her speaking "in a friendly way" to other young men.

The young Benjamin Hudson was poorly educated – even by the standards of the time. His only learning occurred during his very infrequent visits to Sunday School. Locals knew him as a boy who would often mistreat animals.

Eliza Hudson had managed to avoid Benjamin's supervision sufficiently well to take up with other men in the village. She had, for a time, lived with two gentlemen – having a child with each. Eliza also had a child with Benjamin before they married.

The marriage was not to be a happy one. Barely three months had passed before Benjamin deserted his new wife, forcing her to take refuge with their child in the workhouse. Benjamin returned to liberate them just in time to prevent proceedings being taken against him.

Two months later Benjamin was bound over to keep the peace after attacking his wife. He failed to control himself and served three months in prison. Benjamin was released and bound over to keep the peace in respect of his wife for six months. During this period he often threatened her and "dragged her about" but managed to fall short of more severe violence. The moment the six month period was completed he began attacking Eliza again.

In October 1872, Eliza made the decision to take up a position in domestic service in Sheffield and escape Benjamin's clutches. She made the mistake of visiting relatives the day before her new employment was due to commence.

Benjamin paid her a visit. He convinced her that he would change his ways. Eliza relented and moved back to live with her husband. Benjamin quickly reverted to his usual behaviour towards Eliza. The threats escalated into attacks. Eliza was struck so hard that she had to seek medical attention.

Eliza felt compelled to leave the marital home. She disappeared for four days. The two children that the Hudsons now had were looked after by neighbours. Eliza did return but only to much more argument and a final parting. Their sparse furniture was sold and Benjamin was summonsed to appear before Magistrates.

He was forced to pay Eliza five shillings a week from his wages earned whilst working at the colliery in nearby Unstone. He failed to make the payments. He did manage one shilling for one week – but he lost most of his wages at a rabbit coursing event in Sheffield.

Throughout this turbulent period Benjamin made frequent threats to murder Eliza – and occasionally to mete out the same treatment to her mother!

Neighbours later testified that, whatever faults Eliza may have had, idleness was not one of them. She continued to work as hard as she could to try and provide for her children.

Benjamin and Eliza Hudson were to meet up once more, fatefully, at the country stile recently repaired by John Walker near Bowden Lane at Middle Handley.

Benjamin claimed that as they argued, Eliza attempted to hit him with a stone bottle. She actually missed, the bottle smashing on the ground. He admitted that, "in passion", he ripped a hedge-stake from the stile and "beat her with it about the head".

Eliza was discovered and taken to the Devonshire Arms. Josiah Court, physician and surgeon of Staveley was called to examine the body. He noted the severe injuries to her head and face and concluded that they would have been caused by "some heavy instrument". He noticed other injuries – cuts rather than damage from blows. The hedge-stake had been found in the field nearby. It had been broken into three pieces.

Benjamin Hudson made no attempt to conceal his guilt. When asked about Eliza's fate he had replied – "Yes, I believe I am the man".

When asked what had possessed him to do what he had done, he replied –

" Well it was her own bringing on. I met her at the stile and asked her a few questions and she would not give me a straightforward answer. So I thought I would straighten her then."

When a man who had been working nearby asked why he did not hear Eliza cry out, Hudson explained – "No, I stopped her from that at first !"

The Devonshire Arms,
Middle Handley.

The shocking events stirred the public imagination. The local colliers would not have needed much encouragement to take the law into their own hands. There was a genuine possibility that Hudson would have been lynched if he had been present at the original inquest at the Devonshire Arms.

Many believed that Benjamin Hudson had brought shame on their "calling and locality". The levels of anger and indignation rose as the news spread that Eliza was carrying the couple's third child as she had been battered to death.

Hudson was brought before the Magistrates. A large and menacing crowd had already gathered before the accused's cab arrived. Hudson alighted and did not seem to appreciate the seriousness of his position. He was laughing and joking with Police and fellow prisoners as he was escorted into an ante-room to await his hearing.

Hudson treated proceedings with an air of indifference. He was remanded to Derby Gaol until his next hearing as Chesterfield did not have "proper accommodation" for his detention. Hudson was handcuffed and led out to a waiting cab. When faced with the crowd he raised his manacled wrists above his head and clapped his hands. His actions prompted cries of "turn the cab over" although no-one did !

There were rather more elaborate security arrangements in place for Hudson's next court appearance at Chesterfield's Municipal Hall. The area around Chesterfield Railway Station was thronged with people eager to catch a glimpse of Benjamin Hudson as he was transported from Derby. They would be disappointed. Hudson had been removed from the train at Clay Cross, a few miles south. Hudson had been smuggled into Chesterfield by cab.

When Hudson was led into court, his brother and other relatives were visibly distressed. For the first time Hudson's air of bravado appeared under strain. He seemed to become aware of the gravity of the situation he found himself in.

The hearing was quick. Facts were well-established and uncontested. Hudson was sent for trail at the next Derby Assizes. A ruse was utilised to spirit Hudson out of Chesterfield in safety. A cab was brought to the "private" entrance of the Municipal Hall by the Police.

The crowd waiting at the front gate saw this manoeuvre and moved forward to pack the private courtyard. Two policemen then quietly closed the gates. Hudson was safely escorted to a second cab on the opposite side of the road. He was gone before the crowd realised what had happened.

Fortunately for the Police and all concerned, the crowd seemed to "rather enjoy the joke".

Whilst incarcerated at Derby, Hudson's behaviour did nothing to generate any sympathy. He was reluctant to engage with the Prison Chaplain in reflecting on his actions. He rarely spoke and showed no feeling for the fate that had befallen Eliza. He never showed any remorse.

On the eve of his execution Hudson refused to see a party of twelve of his relatives. He did, though, request that some letters be written on his behalf to his few remaining friends. He was still unable to read or write.

On the Sunday afternoon before Hudson's execution a "respectable lady" from Derby presented herself at Derby Gaol and, to great astonishment, asked to see the prisoner. She informed the Chaplain that it was "borne in upon her by the Spirit" that she must see Hudson. Moreover, she asserted that she could "do him good".

The lady maintained an air of plausibility and was granted a meeting with the Governor. She told him that she had powers that would "unlock men's hearts". She did not prevail upon the Governor and was turned away.

Monday morning – the appointed time for the execution of Benjamin Hudson – duly arrived. A late, and rather half-hearted, appeal to the Home Secretary for clemency had proved fruitless. Hudson, for his part, had been saying to warders for several days that he just wanted to be hanged. He was granted his wish.

CHAPTER EIGHTEEN

'Shog' Seen off by Reverend Nodder

Marsh Green Hall is situated just outside the picturesque village of Ashover. In 1857, on a cold and dark February night , this peaceful home was interrupted by a series of violent and dramatic events.

The occupants of the Hall had retired to bed. The Reverend John Nodder was fast asleep in his apartment at the rear of the building. His wife and their seven-week-old baby were settled in the front bedroom. The Reverend Nodder's niece, Marianne Heeley, was staying with the family and she was in a neighbouring bedroom.

Mrs Nodder was awakened by a noise from outside. She opened the curtains and was confronted with a strange face very close to the window pane. Mrs Nodder was startled and frightened but reacted with commendable calm as she stood in her nightdress.

Mrs Nodder quickly drew back the curtains, put on her slippers, lifted the baby out of the cot and made for the door.

As Mrs Nodder was leaving the room the lower six panels of the bedroom window were smashed and part of the frame collapsed. Two men entered, they had managed to use a ladder that they had found in the stock yard below.

Mrs Nodder managed to close the door and had the presence of mind to hold it long enough to lock it. She then made good her escape down the corridor which led to her husband's room. The intruders were equipped with a crowbar. They were quickly able to make a big enough hole to reach through and grab the key from the outside. They moved on to the next room.

Marianne Heeley had been disturbed by the commotion and heard the men approach. She braced herself against her door and managed to buy herself sufficient time to plan her escape. Bravely, Marianne headed for the window. She climbed out, clad only in her nightgown, and dangled herself

Ashover – a picturesque village.

outside – her fingers gradually slipping from the window sill. Her room was 14 feet above the yard below. Her grip could not hold and fell. Despite injuring her back, Marianne struggled to her feet and ran barefoot to nearby Ashover to summon help.

Mrs Nodder, by this time, had found refuge with her husband – again locking the door behind her. Reverend Nodder was out of bed and armed with a pair of large "horse pistols" which he kept loaded on top of a cupboard.

Voices were heard outside the room – "Now lads, come on, they're here!" Reverend Nodder replied, giving full notice of his intent – "If you enter here I'll shoot you!"

Reverend Nodder's threat was disregarded. The first intruder burst in. He was dressed in a woman's black gown and wore a mask – he was not carrying a weapon but held a flickering candle in his left hand. At this point the resourceful Mrs Nodder decided that the safest strategy was compliance. Her advice to her husband was "give them what they want or they'll murder us !"

Reverend Nodder, in some respect, followed his wife's thinking. Uttering the words – "I'll give you what you want !" – he took two paces back and fired one of his pistols. The shot hit the first man in the abdomen.

The intruders rapidly turned around and hurtled back along the corridor. As they ran, particles of shot fell from the wounded man's clothing. They retraced their steps into Mrs Nodders's bedroom and launched themselves through the window, taking with them any remaining splinters of glass and woodwork. Their exit was too hasty to include the ladder. They tumbled the same distance as Marianne Heeley and ended up in a heap in the yard below. They scrambled to their feet and continued their headlong escape.

Reverend Nodder lost no time in sounding the alarm. His task was made easier because a dozen men were already on their way from Ashover, having been alerted by the hobbling Marianne Heeley. The search for the gang began in earnest.There was a trail of blood from the wounded man and, also, from other gang members who had been injured by the glass as the jumped through the upstairs window. The large and menacing Marsh Green Hall guard dog was located – fast asleep. It had been drugged and had not been capable of raising the alarm.

The direction of the gang's escape was clear for all to see. Footprints led across the flower garden to small piles of discarded clothing. The number of dresses, gowns and masks indicated that the gang had, at least, four members.

Despite all these clues, and the speed of the response, the members of the gang were not apprehended by the authorities at the scene. The Police did manage to gather information about the route taken by the unfortunate burglars. A butcher travelling from Wirksworth to Chesterfield Market met a man at Kelstedge whose leg was bandaged and swollen. The man also appeared to have cuts to his hands as he asked the tradesman for a ride into Chesterfield. He offered a shilling in payment.

The butcher was a little suspicious about the condition of his new passenger. He enquired about the man's wounds and, at first, was told that they had been sustained as the result of a robbery. However, the man changed his original story and said that he had been involved in a prize fight which carried a purse of £50!

The injured man was deposited in Chesterfield. He was seen to try to clean himself up at the White Horse Inn and then make his way to Chesterfield Station, where he bought a ticket to Derby.

It soon emerged that Marsh Green Hall, although the largest and most appealing, had been far from the only target. A gang had been operating in the area for a number days. These gentlemen, known as "ticket of leave men", had only partly served sentences in the penal colonies in Australia. They had returned, not to reform, but with the intention of scouring the countryside to rob any house which seemed worthy of the effort. They often carried firearms and always used a number of disguises.

At Wingerworth they had entered the house of Joseph Trickett, a retired soldier. They were able to easily remove a number of articles including several pieces of furniture. Joseph Trickett had received an injury in battle and was totally deaf. The gang were able to take their time

The church in Ashover.

and move on undetected.

Mr Hill, a farmer in Walton, discovered that he was missing some fowls and a pitchfork. A neighbour discovered a number of tiles had been removed from his roof – but he had gained the pitchfork which the gang had jettisoned in favour of better booty.

THE DERBYSHIRE TIMES.

BURGLARY AT ASHOVER.
ONE OF THE BURGLARS SHOT.

A burglary occurred between one and two o'clock on Saturday morning last, at the residence of the Rev. J Nodder, Marsh Green, Ashover, about eight miles from Chesterfield. The house stands in a secluded place

Burglary at Ashover – Derbyshire Times *28 February 1857.*

The gang continued their work in Walton. They entered a house in the dead of night and crept upstairs to where the occupants were asleep. Quietly, they managed to rob a couple of four shillings from their pockets and a much larger sum of three pounds and sixpence from a bedroom drawer. However, they had some difficulty when the couple's daughter awoke and called out for her father. One of the robbers was bold enough to enter her room and pretend to be her father. He asked what she wanted and provided her with some water as she was feeling unwell. He reassured her about any noise that she may have heard and, quietly, left.

The Police, slow to make an arrest in Derbyshire, were methodical and determined in the following days. They believed that the "ticket of leave" men had contacts in Nottingham and Birmingham. Indeed, part of a Birmingham newspaper had been found in an outbuilding close to Marsh Green Hall.

A group of five men had been seen in and around Ashover the evening before the attempted burglary at Reverend Nodder's home. Descriptions and evidence led the Police to believe that the wounded man, and ringleader, was a man known as "Shogg". He had, indeed, recently returned to Birmingham from penal servitude in Australia.

The Police were very clever in the way they sought out "Shogg" in Birmingham. They visited known contacts of the criminal fraternity who were capable of providing medical assistance. Sure enough an injured man was located in a woman's house as she was applying a number of leeches to a badly sprained ankle. The "patient" was also suffering from "shot marks, inflammation and lacerations below the stomach."

"Shogg" was duly arrested and stood trial at Derby Assizes on Thursday 19 March 1857 under his real name of Thomas Wooton. He was sentenced to twenty-five years transportation to the penal colonies in Australia!

"Shogg" greeted his sentence with a wry smile.

CHAPTER NINETEEN
A Life of Crime is Hard

In 1863, John Wilson found himself facing justice at the hands of Chesterfield Magistrates. He had attempted to keep hunger at bay by stealing a jar of marmalade. He begged for leniency but was sentenced to seven days hard labour.

Hard labour was a common feature of Victorian justice. Sometimes the guilty were obliged to work on roads and other community projects but more often it was an institutional sanction.

Victorian gaols used some practices that were designed to be purely punitive. "Shot drill" was simple and mindless. Prisoners were required to pick up a cannonball and move it three paces to the left and place it on the ground. It was then lifted up again and carried three paces to the right. This sequence repeated itself seemingly endlessly.

The crank machine was equally demoralising. Convicts stood on paddles and moved large cups through sand. Prison Officers adjusted screws to make resistance greater and the task more onerous – and gained a new nickname in the process.

Treadmills, by comparison, were rather productive. The effort of the prisoners was converted into energy to grind corn, pump water or provide ventilation.

The picking of oakum was physically less demanding but difficult, tedious and painful. Tired sore hands bled as the fibres of heavy tarred rope were carefully pulled apart. These "liberated" strands were then reworked to make an invaluable resource. The Royal Navy used vast quantities to caulk their wooden warships. The English language, again, expanded a little as "money for old rope" explained this business of recycling.

Prisoners dealt with by the Chesterfield Magistrates were taken to Derby Gaol to undertake their hard labour. The two activities used were the treadmill and the picking of oakum.

Picking oakum.

At the time of John Wilson's marmalade theft, a master baker supervised fifty-two prisoners' toil on Derby's treadmill. Fourteen others were spending the majority of their daylight hours picking oakum. The day for all began before six o'clock in the morning.

At the time, Wilson's sentence was not particularly harsh. Mary Smith, alias the "Brampton Angel", received a months hard labour for being "drunk and riotous" in Brampton at two o'clock on a Sunday afternoon.

The Chesterfield Magistrates seemed to show some level of consistency. Zillah Dawes, a young Chesterfield woman of "unfortunate class", was charged with using indecent language on Low Pavement. This was serious enough to attract the attention of Constable Windle. Unfortunately for Zillah she did not move on as requested. Worse still, she knocked Windle's hat off. Zillah's behaviour triggered a sentence of one month of hard labour.

The theft of a whip in Hasland attracted the same tariff as Mary Smith, Zillah Dawes and John Wilson. George Warren would serve his month of hard labour even though the whip was valued at the considerable sum of twelve shillings and sixpence – much more than the jar of marmalade.

The value of the objects stolen could not always give an indication of the term of hard labour. Elizabeth Edeson stole a purse containing six shillings. She was to be asked to labour a month … for each shilling!

In the middle of the nineteenth century begging was not viewed at all sympathetically. George Taylor and James Gardner had been going from house to house in Brampton. They were apprehended by Constable Hawkins who found that they had, between them, seven pence and a small quantity of bread. The two gentlemen would not have to worry about food and shelter for twenty-one days as they began their stint of hard labour.

A similar sentence was given to a fitter from Dronfield and a collier from Whittington Moor. They were guilty of committing an " indecent nuisance" by urinating in Church Alley near the Cross Keys public house. In addition to their twenty-one days hard labour they were each fined ten shillings and made to pay costs.

Victorian society's view of decency and appropriate behaviour can clearly be identified in the utilisation of hard labour sentences. James Silcock received three months for being "idle, disorderly and neglecting to maintain his wife and family." Matthew Ryan, described in Court as "a gentleman from Ireland" received two months hard labour for his ill treatment of another lady. Bridget Murphy had left her home in Froggatts Yard to collect water when Ryan, a neighbour, rushed towards her and spat in her face.

Magistrates,occasionally, were more thoughtful and creative in their sentencing. Elizabeth Heathcote, a fourteen-year-old servant, had pleaded guilty to "gaining by false pretences three dresses and various other items."

Time and trouble was taken to make enquiries about Elizabeth's background. It became apparent that the girl had been deserted in early childhood. The Magistrates decided that one months imprisonment was appropriate. However, on release Elizabeth was to be sent to a Reformatory for four years. It was hoped that she would have the opportunity to be "restored to society and make her way in the world respectably."

A heavy reliance on pure hard labour did, however, continue for many years. Some sentences were very lengthy considering the physical strain involved. George Bradbury, a watchmaker, who had misappropriated the property of customers, received eighteen months.

John Green, a twenty-two year old hawker, was sentenced to two years hard labour. Green had "received" a drake, three ducks and two hens which had all been stolen from Mary Jebb of Walton.

Hard labour remained a feature of British justice until it was abolished in 1948. Some lamented its passing. Sir William Darling, the M.P. for

Edinburgh, made his position clear – "The abolition of hard labour will be a refinement of cruelty. I can think of nothing more cruel than to confine a man to the limits of his cell, day-in day-out, without any occupation whatsoever."

A snapshot of society in New Square, Chesterfield.

CHAPTER TWENTY

Garrotting Comes to Town!

In 1862 garrotting appeared to be endemic on Britain's streets. This was not the specific means of execution favoured by the Spanish. It was street robbery that often involved the grabbing of the victim's neck.

The nation was in fear of this crime. *The Times* newspaper was calling for harsh penalties after an M.P. was "garrotted" in London on his way home from a late sitting at the House of Commons.

Gentlemen were urged to purchase "life preservers" – heavy coshes made from lead – to fend off would-be garrotters. Victorian inventors went a stage further and began to design steel spiked collars to be worn around the neck.

In November 1862 there was an "anti-garrotting club" which met in Derby. One of the gentlemen present, Mr Buckland, was pleased to demonstrate his cleverly designed gloves. These looked like ordinary "dog skin" gloves but concealed a pair of sharpened curved steel hooks. The hooks resembled "the size and shape of a parrot's claw". Mr Buckland advised a victim to grab the garrotter's arm and inflict "such wounds as would cause the garrotter to speedily release his hold."

"Garrotting" was regularly used as a term to describe criminal activity in Derbyshire in the 1860s. In Chesterfield, Henry Moore was to shock respectable society by "garrotting" two separate victims on the same day.

Moore's first victim was William Dwight, a gamekeeper employed by a local gentleman, Mr R. Bellyse Esq. Dwight had called in to The Waggon, a public house kept by John Silcock on Wheeldon Lane.

Dwight remained in The Waggon from mid-afternoon until six-thirty in the evening. He freely admitted that he "might have had a share of eight or nine pints at Silcocks and three pints before." Henry Moore and George Wetton were present as Dwight was enjoying a game of skittles. At one stage, Dwight had given a bystander five shillings to hold whilst he played.

Dwight decided to leave. Once outside he paused to count his money

A garrotte robbery.

– he had "five pounds in gold and two pounds in silver". Moore and Wetton also left The Waggon and quickly caught up with Dwight.

Henry Moore confronted Dwight and demanded his money. Dwight yelled "murder!". Moore responded by telling his accomplice to "put your finger down his throat and stop his rattle!" These were the last words that their victim recalled hearing before being knocked unconscious. When Dwight came round his pockets were empty.

Encouraged by this success, Moore moved on to his second victim. Thomas Biggin left The Spinning Wheel on Glumangate and walked past a man leaning on the wall next to the bay window of the public house. The man was Henry Moore.

Biggin soon had the feeling that he was being followed by two men. He speeded up – they increased their pace and gradually closed the distance. Biggin had reached Station Road and decided to stop and let the men walk past.

Moore took the opportunity to pin Biggin up against the wall. Biggin, like Dwight, yelled "murder!". Moore grabbed Biggin by the throat and the other man gave the victim "a chuck up under the chin".

Some locals, alerted, by Biggin's cry arrived just in time to hear the change jingling as Moore rifled Biggin's pockets. The two assailants ran off having relieved Biggin of three shillings and sixpence.

Henry Moore, George Wetton and Robert Turner were soon caught. They were found guilty of robbing their victims and given severe sentences. All three were given penal servitude with Moore receiving fourteen years, Wetton ten years and Turner seven years.

The *Derbyshire Times* reflected the feelings of shock and outrage, finding it "alarming that ...in a thickly populated and closely built town like Chesterfield there should have been two such garrotting incidents in the same night."

The treatment of "garrotters" reflected the anxiety society felt about this kind of crime. In Leeds eight garrotters avoided gaol but were, instead, given over two thousand lashes of the cat o'nine tails between them. The ordeal lasted just under an hour and occupied a team of four warders non-stop.

The wealthy clearly felt at risk and a daring garrotte robbery at Derby in 1865 did little to reassure them. Mr Samuel Walker Cox Esq. was robbed by George Callaghan, a tailor, and George Clarke, a collier. Mr Cox was the brother of W.T. Cox the Member of Parliament for Derby. Such an attack was sure to be pursued vigorously by the authorities.

Callaghan and Clarke were caught and put on trial. They decided to conduct their own defence but it was always going to be an uphill task. Callaghan was sentenced to fifteen years penal servitude and Clarke to twelve.

In the Derby garrotting a silver watch had been stolen. Every effort was made to recover this item. Eventually, two years later a local shoemaker, Thomas Madden was charged with receiving the stolen watch. He was sentenced to six months imprisonment.

Garrotting was seen a threat to the established order of Victorian society. It was not merely the preserve of Derbyshire towns. In December 1863, in the early days of the national frenzy, John Quinn was sentenced to four years penal servitude. Quinn had held Robert Mellor by the neck in Taddington "with intent to enable two persons unknown to steal a purse and two half sovereigns."

An anti-garotting collar.

CHAPTER TWENTY-ONE
A Crystal, a Few Wild Beasts and a Slap in the Face with a Fish

Victorian children were sometimes in need of admonishment. In 1863, William Galsthorpe went too far when he saw fit to discipline young Edward Harvey at Hasland. He admitted to the local magistrates that he had given the youngster a "few smart strokes".

Mr Maynard, passing judgement, said that he did not blame a person for "properly correcting " a boy – but it ought not be done savagely. He had inspected Edward's back and was of the opinion that Galsthorpe had used too much violence. Galsthorpe was fined two shillings and sixpence and ordered to pay costs.

In the same year, Samuel Darwin, aged ten, was up before the Court in Derby. Samuel had stabbed boy by the name of Flinders. The magistrates were keen to fully understand the circumstances leading up to the stabbing which, fortunately, did not prove fatal. They employed a thorough and inventive approach to their questioning as they sought a motive:

Dr Peach, Magistrate, addresses Samuel Darwin – "Had you won any of his marbles ?"

Samuel – "No sir."

Dr Peach – "Had you quarrelled ?"

Samuel – " No sir. I was playing in a cart and he said he would kill me. He hit me with a brick-end."

The Bench clearly believed that this was a sufficient level of provocation. Darwin was discharged with a reprimand and told he "must never use a knife again."

A boy from New Whittington demonstrated something akin to Darwin's penchant for danger. In 1863 Gilbert Wragg was in school, but not fully concentrating on the lesson. He was fiddling with "powder and matches", which were concealed in his trouser pocket. The outcome was as predictable as it was painful. Gilbert set himself alight and was "severely burnt about the thigh, abdomen and hand."

Gilbert's antics were not regarded as being especially unusual at the time. He was the fourth boy "injured by powder" in New Whittington that week!

Football made a social impact beyond the activities of the more organised teams that the area could now boast. In December 1898 there was a keenly contested local "derby" between Old Brampton and Brampton United. It was a fast and exciting game with Old Brampton leading by the only goal. Brampton United, though, "did not like the beating" and left the field ten minutes before time !

In 1888, a "cowardly assault" was reported at a football match involving Clay Cross Town and Staveley Olympic. The confrontation did not involve players. John Dronfield of High Street in Clay Cross attempted to watch the game without paying. He was confronted by Edward Crossland who was on the gate. Dronfield struck Crossland very hard –

Picturesque Bakewell, an unlikely setting for a visit by Bostocks's Wild Beast Show.

the unfortunate gateman had to be carried home, and was unable to work for three weeks.

The popularity of the sport was leading to many spontaneous games which the local press labelled "the football nuisance". Six local colliers were brought to court charged with "playing football on the highway". The offenders' ages ranged from twenty years to thirteen years of age. They were all treated harshly – each being fined the considerable sum of ten shillings. They were given the alternative of seven days imprisonment!

Frederick Cutts, another local footballer, was also to receive a stiff sentence. Cutts had been playing football in Clay Cross and, along with the rest of his team, had been transported there by "brake". Unfortunately, their driver went home without them and the gentlemen found themselves stranded.

Cutts and his team-mates found some solace by visiting most of the public houses in Clay Cross. At the Angel Inn Cutts decided to steal a bicycle belonging to the landlady.

Cutts managed to negotiate the journey to Tibshelf and, around midnight, sold the bicycle to the local blacksmith, Edward Godfrey. Godfrey paid a guinea for the bicycle – probably a bargain as it was later valued at five pounds by its owner.

Godfrey was a little curious about the circumstances leading up to the transaction but was reassured by Cutts. The latter explained that the bicycle belonged to his sister but she couldn't ride it. Godfrey, very reasonably, said that if Cutts were to change his mind he would be willing to sell the bicycle back to him. Cutts replied "I don't think I shall fetch it back."

When the theft came to light Cutts claimed that he was so drunk that he couldn't remember anything. Superintendent Eyre pointed out that if he had been that drunk Cutts would never have made it to Tibshelf on a bicycle in the dark. Cutts was sent down to Derby Gaol for "three weeks hard".

Pastimes other than football provoked criminal behaviour. In 1863 Thomas Fox was charged with shooting a pigeon. Henry Heeson, the pigeon's owner heard a shot one Sunday morning, he looked up just in time to see his bird plummet to the ground. Fox admitted shooting the pigeon but said that there had been a great deal of "pigeon flying" and this was causing a "great nuisance".

Fox said that he saw a pigeon fly past and shot it not knowing whether it was tame or wild. Mr Maynard, the Magistrate, felt that the status of the bird was irrelevant and Fox was ordered to pay one shilling (the value of the pigeon) plus a fine of two shillings and sixpence plus costs – or face seven days imprisonment.

Wildlife did not always need human intervention to suffer harm. In 1869 "Bostock's Wild Beast Show " visited Bakewell. It more than lived up to its billing.

One evening, just before the official Wild Beast Show was due to begin a hyena "ferociously" attacked a wolf. The wolf's leg was broken in two places.

The hyena attack caused such a commotion that three black bears and another hyena became over-excited. They "howled and leaped about in a frantic manner". The noise alarmed local residents.

Peace was eventually restored. Mr Leach, the local veterinary surgeon arrived on the scene. He was forced to amputate the leg of the injured wolf.

The following day Bostock's Wild Beast Show left Bakewell and was happy to report that the wolf "was doing well" !

During the same week the peace and tranquillity of Chapel-en-le Frith was shattered. George Sweatmore of New Mills was charged with assaulting Sergeant Swallow. The Police Officer had been called to deal with Sweatmore because the prisoner had been "insulting some excursionists by striking them in the face with a piece of fish."

Sweatmore had been found in a drunken state and using bad language. When cornered by Sergeant Swallow he "stripped himself" before launching an attack on the officer.

Sweatmore was sentenced to one month's hard labour at Derby Gaol.

Society did not always have to rely upon courts of law to lay down the parameters of acceptable social behaviour. The *Derbyshire Times* of May 1869 was to report, in some detail, the cautionary tale of "A faithless wife serenaded".

It appeared that a "Tibshelf wife" had left her husband and children to take up with a "gay young bachelor". She was, it was claimed, "weary of the monotony of household duties".

Sadly, the new and exciting relationship was to prove short-lived. The lady was forced to return to her husband who received her "with ready welcome".

The female population of Tibshelf proved to be less forgiving. It was decided to gather in numbers and serenade the returning wife with songs. The lyrics made it clear to all that her recent lapse was viewed as an affront to respectable society.

For several days a procession of women and boys marched around the village. The boys formed a band, banging on tin kettles, to accompany the impromptu female choir. To add to the spectacle, effigies of the errant wife and her paramour were paraded to the delight of bystanders.

Fortune tellers fared little better than unfaithful wives. In 1880 Levi Cooke faced Magistrates in Chesterfield. He was accused of being "a rogue and vagabond" who had charged the unsuspecting public for some dubious insights into the future.

Cooke had upset one gentleman by predicting the sudden death of his wife – which had proved, thus far, incorrect. Cooke also had informed another man that he would be blessed with seven children. The fact that this man was unmarried, at the time, helped to bring the originator of this insight before the Magistrates.

The case against Levi Cooke was further strengthened by the sad passing of a lady that had consulted him. It was believed that Cooke's "art" and use of sorcery had affected her to such an extent that she had died from a "shock to her nervous system".

Cooke's arrival in Court was not reported sympathetically in the local press. The *Derby Mercury* described him as "a tall dark complexioned man, unusually ignorant even for a fortune teller, repulsively foul in appearance, and about the last man in the world that one would think could read a school primer, much less the stars and planets and the futures of man or woman."

The Court took great delight in examining the "crystal" apparatus that Cooke used to see into the future. On closer examination Cooke's "crystal ball" was revealed as being the oval stopper from a wine decanter. The Clerk of the Court and others were charged with the task of peering into the glass and reporting any revelations. To the amusement of onlookers all declared that nothing could be seen.

Cooke was found guilty and sentenced to three months with hard labour. The Magistrates, rather like the female population of Tibshelf, had put down a marker. The summing up of the case was clear – "It is much to be wished that not only fortune tellers in lanes and garrets but inspirational trance mediums, clairvoyants and sham necromancers should all have their nefarious practices exposed and punished as they justly deserve."

CHAPTER TWENTY-TWO
A Ghostly Murder in the Shambles

Nowadays organised ghost walks visit the area of Chesterfield known as the "Shambles". They seek a glimpse of the spectre of George Collis.

The body of George Collis was discovered by chance in August 1846. Mr Bunting, a local corn dealer, had employed two local men to empty and clean out a cesspit that served his property in Falcon Yard. It was a particularly unpleasant task as two privies fed directly into the pit.

Some remains were located as the contents were slowly removed. At first, it was believed that they were dealing with the body of a sheep. However, the discovery of clothing indicated that the remains were, most probably, human.

The body was in a sorry state, as it was lifted out "three parts fell away". The bones were then laid out on a grassy area that belonged to Mr Bunting. They appeared to those of a man, aged between twenty and thirty years of age.

The distinctive clothing confirmed that the remains of twenty-six-year old George Collis had been found. When he was last seen, on Sunday 7 December 1845 he had been wearing a bright yellow waistcoat – this was still intact.

George had visited his girlfiend, Ellen Beresford, just prior to his disappearance and the pair had exchanged garters. George, therefore was wearing an odd pair – one white and one red. It was the latter that Ellen had given him. These two garters were still attached to the remains found in Falcon Yard – as was a handkerchief which had been embroidered with the initials "G.C." by Ellen.

It was also straightforward to identify how George Collis had met his end. A battered hat, still with the body, was consistent with a serious fracture to his skull.

At first, locals were surprised to discover the body was that of George

The Shambles Chesterfield the scene of the murder of George Collis. Note the "fleshamols" of the butchers' shops. These flaps were used to prepare and display meat. The murderer John Platts ran a shop here.

Collis. It had been generally believed that Collis had gone to Manchester in search of work. He had informed Ellen Beresford of his plans, perhaps prompting the exchange of garters as a keepsake until his return. He had also informed his mother of his plans and told her not to expect any communication for a short while.

Soon, though, memories began to stir People began to recall a number of strange events that had occurred in December 1845.

Noises had been heard outside a butcher's shop run by John Platts. Platts, locally known as "Gog" was twenty-two years of age, of "stout" build and only four feet eleven inches in height. George Collis had started working with Platts when his former occupation as a gentleman's servant at Hasland Hall had come to an end.

Collis had loaned Platts some money, which had not been repaid. This caused tension in their relationship. A Sunday evening meeting was arranged to try to resolve matters between the two men. Platts was determined that any resolution would be upon his terms. Platts and Henry Morley, another butcher from nearby Packers Row, decided that they would murder George Collis.

Collis did not appear to appreciate the seriousness of his position. He willingly joined the two conspirators in a tour of local inn, finally arriving at the Old Angel. Later, all three were seen by numerous witnesses making their way to Platt's shop.

Samuel Slack, on his way to the Bulls Head, recalled how one of the men seemed to be pushed into Platt's premises. This man appeared to Slack to be either "drunken" or "stupefied".

A number of noises resulted in a small crowd gathering outside. There was concern for the welfare of Hannah, the girlfriend of John Platts, as thuds and groans were clearly heard. Thomas Harvey, a local shoemaker, recalled the first blow that he heard. It was, he remembers, a "heavy" strike – not "struck against a block or a board but a softer substance".

Harvey shouted that he believed that there was "murder in Platts!". The others present did not share his level of concern. Thomas Bellamy shouted through the door to Platts – asking him to explain what was going on. Platts reassured those outside that he had merely consumed too much rum and was feeling very sick. This, in combination with a reliable sighting of Hannah at a church service, resulted in the gathering drifting back to their usual Sunday evening patronage of the local alehouses.

Soon afterwards, John Heathcote, a local man, saw Platts, Morley and another unidentified man carrying what appeared to be a bundle towards the Falcon Yard. Platts was next seen in the Old Angel where he went for another drink. He had a blood stained bandage on his right hand. When Catherine Franks, the landlady, enquired about his injury Platts said that he had caught himself on a hook.

As soon as the body of George Collis was discovered Platts was arrested. Henry Morley was soon out of the clutches of British justice. Three days after the inquest was held relating to Collis, Morley was dead. He was already in a "state of delirium" brought upon by the after effects of typhus.

Platts, of course, denied having any part in the murder of George Collis. He tried to embellish stories of him going to Manchester. At one point, he even claimed that he had, recently, seen Collis driving a cab.

The Shambles today.

The Royal Oak in the Shambles – a twelfth-century inn close to the butcher's shop of John Platts.

The Falcon Yard, once the site of a cesspit containing the body of George Collis.

The case against Platts, already strong, was soon to become overwhelming. The cesspit in the Falcon Yard had yielded all of the unfortunate George Collis apart from his boots, a yellow canvas purse and a watch. All three items were traced back to Platts.

The progress of the watch proved very easy to track. Pawnbrokers tickets showed that Platts's mother had pawned it and redeemed it. Platts claimed that a local character "Lanky Bill" had sold the watch to him. "Lanky Bill" was duly found and wisely denied any dealings with the floundering Platts.

At his trial, Platts continued to profess his innocence. He put forward the theory that Collis may have accidentally fallen into the cesspit. The jury, though, only needed a few minutes to deliberate.

John Platts was found guilty of murder and sentenced to death. Whilst awaiting his execution Platts finally produced a written confession. In it, he admitted planning the murder of Collis but, crucially, he denied striking him. He blamed the deceased Morley and went great lengths to describe how the latter had provided and concealed a spade in order to kill Collis.

In actual fact the jury had been convinced by evidence that the fatal skull fracture had, probably, been caused by a hammer and not a spade. One of the witnesses, John Heathcote, had given testimony that he had seen Platts with a hammer with a long handle and a sharp face – resembling an axe.

On 7 April 1847, at midday, Platts was executed at Derby Gaol. He had requested that no people from Chesterfield be allowed to witness his end. This request was denied. A huge crowd of twenty thousand was in attendance. A good number from Chesterfield swelling the ranks from Derby, Sheffield and Nottingham.

Throughout his trial and his imprisonment, Platts had remained steadfast. However, his resolve was to desert him as he was required to make his way to the scaffold. He had to be supported by his gaolers.

Awaiting John Platts was Samuel Haywood – an experienced hangman. Platts was to be Haywood's fiftieth victim and he had requested heavy leg irons to speed his passage. Once in place, the bolts were swiftly drawn and Platts "struggled much for a short time" before he was pronounced dead.

The large crowd, according to the local press, "behaved decorously". It was noted that fewer females were present than was normal for such an event. Hannah, Platt's girlfriend, had given birth to their child only three weeks previously.

The ghost of the unfortunate George Collis provides a direct link to events on a Derbyshire Sunday evening in 1845.

CHAPTER TWENTY-THREE

Victorian Wedded Bliss…
at a Price!

By the 1870s Chesterfield had already become notorious for riotous weddings involving its "lower classes". In 1874, the marriage of Edward and Jane Barratt at the parish church was to be the precursor of some lively events.

The newly-wed Barratts were residents of Wheeldon Lane. It enjoyed a colourful reputation and bordered the "Yards" and the "Dog Kennels", themselves no strangers to disorder. Wheeldon Lane was described as being the "resort of roughs and low women". A letter to the *Derbyshire Times* in 1875 had gone as far as to compare the conditions there to those encountered by Dr Livingstone as he explored Africa.

The Barratt wedding party had moved on from the church to celebrate in the local taverns before making its way home. By the time the market place was reached, the happy couple had begun to argue quite violently.

Jane Barratt's loud behaviour soon attracted the attention of a police constable. He made no allowance for the fact that she was wearing a wedding dress and attempted to arrest her for drunkenness. At this point, Edward Barratt ceased arguing with his new wife and assumed the role of her steadfast protector. Barratt hit the constable in the face.

A scuffle then ensued between the groom and the officer. A crowd quickly gathered to witness the escalation of events as the groom's brothers and more constables joined the fray.

Jane Barratt participated in the melee. Her bridal outfit was soon the worse for wear – the orange blossom decorations failed to stand up to the rigours of the conflict.

Some semblance of order was restored as most of the wedding party was rounded up and escorted to the Police Station. One gentleman, however, managed to escape and take refuge in the Crown and Cushion nearby. From the relative safety and security of the inn, the man loudly

118

proclaimed that all the policeman in the town would be unable to "take him".

The veracity of his claim was soon put to the test. Superintendent Home entered the Crown and Cushion and grabbed the man by the neck. The policeman was kicked but still managed to drag his quarry into the alleyway and across the market place. He was applauded by bystanders who were impressed that an officer of such seniority should take it upon himself to act so decisively.

Such behaviour was not exclusive to Chesterfield. In 1879, a woman in Derby caused havoc at her son's wedding at Christ Church on Normanton Road. She was vehemently opposed to her son's choice of partner. She stationed herself at the doorway of the church and roundly abused her son and the minister. Hardly drawing

Crown and Cushion at the head of the Yards.

breath she then launched into a stream of "by no means choice epithets" in relation to the bride.

The antics of this angry lady attracted a sizeable crowd. This gathering, largely female, did not approve of her position and a lively debate ensued. The minister seized the opportunity and the doors to the church were quickly shut to allow the ceremony to continue.

Outside, events were simmering. There was much "throwing of arms and headgear".

Wisely, the newlyweds were smuggled out of a side vestry door. They were able to make good their escape – a matter of seconds before the crowd sensed an opportunity and began to move in.

In 1881, St Barholomew's church in Clay Cross was the scene of some more marital mayhem. The Reverend F.J. Metcalfe was attempting to conduct the marriage ceremony but was constantly interrupted by the bridegroom. The latter was using "disreputable language" throughout and, on more than one occasion, asked Rev. Metcalfe "to be bloody sharp and get it done !".

Rev. Metcalfe refused to continue and walked out of the church. His departure caused much wailing on the part of the bride who ran after him and begged him to return. Metcalfe refused and took refuge in the Vicarage next door.

Negotiations were eventually successful and Rev. Metcalfe returned. The bridegroom explained his behaviour – but in a rather unsatisfactory fashion. He claimed that his antics were the result of a wager between himself and a fellow workman!

A second wedding that same day at St Bartholomew's was delayed as the carriage containing the wedding party overturned. Thankfully, there were no serious injuries – although the unfortunate Rev. Metcalfe was not yet clear of wedding related mishaps.

In 1883, the good Reverend was the victim of a "disgraceful hoax". The celebration of the Holy Communion was going according to plan until the wine was poured into the silver cup. The wine had, somehow, become ink. The previous day there had been a number of weddings. Metcalfe was convinced that some of the guests were responsible for the switch.

An eventful Victorian wedding ceremony was not always the end of marital drama and strife. Divorce was one means of resolving insur-mountable differences. Another was the sale of a wife.

This rather extreme stategy was not unusual in Derbyshire. In 1855, a man led his wife around Derby market with a halter placed around her waist. The unfortunate lady was offered for sale. Eventually a bargain was struck – the wife being exchanged for eighteen pence and a quart of ale.

In 1873 a man from Belper headed for America in order to escape his mounting debts. A week later all his goods were put up for sale to try to pay off his creditors. "Lot 29" aroused considerable interest. The abandoned wife was led around Belper market place, again with halter around her waist.

A large crowd gathered to witness this sad spectacle. The local press were in no doubt that the woman was "a disgrace to her sex" but public opinion appeared to be even more indignant regarding the person who had actually put the halter on and led her around. There was regret expressed that some "nailers", a reference to a traditional Belper trade, did not take action and give him "a round dozen well laid on with the rope's end".

Lot 29 did not find a buyer.

The Market Hall, Chesterfield.

Alfreton, in 1882, saw two, rather more, successful transactions. First, John Wilson, a collier sold his wife for fourpence. The second was a little more complex.

One Saturday night a man and his wife were drinking in a public house in Alfreton. They were in the company of the son of the landlord of their lodging house. The woman and the young man were becoming over familiar. At first the husband was jealous but soon changed his position. He offered to sell his wife to the younger man for the price of a glass of ale. His wife was keen that the offer be accepted and removed her wedding ring the moment that the drink was produced. There had been an alternative offer of "tuppence" from an interested onlooker but this had been rejected . The "new" couple finished their drinks and departed, not only the inn, but also the town!

By 1893, in Chesterfield, the practice of selling a wife had moved towards more formal arrangements. A man had agreed to sell his wife to a collier. The trio met with the woman's father and two family friends to thrash out suitable terms. A fee of thirty shillings was agreed and a bill of sale contained the buyer's name followed by the words "to have my wife Elizabeth free from me for ever to do as she has mind this day , December 11th 1893."

At least, by the end of the nineteenth century, the use of a halter was no longer deemed appropriate.

CHAPTER TWENTY-FOUR

Froggatts Yard and the Dog Kennels

Nowadays, the Yards in Chesterfield is a pleasant gentrified area. Cafés and craft shops jostle for footfall that is channelled along narrow winding alleyways. The signage for "Falcon Yard ", "Theatre Yard" and "Wards Yard" are reminders of a bygone age.

Life was hard in Victorian Chesterfield. The Yards were the centre of much crime, depravity and desperation. Two locations dominate the stories of the time – Froggatts Yard and the Dog Kennels.

Froggatts Yard used to run south from Low Pavement, at its head was once the Bird in Hand public house. The Bird in Hand was demolished to make space for the new Portland Hotel – as part of development that would include the Lancashire, Derby and East Coast Railway Station.

The area had a claim to notoriety as early as 1788. The infamous William Deacon Brodie sent John Tasker, the landlord of the Bird in Hand, two trunks full of silks for "storage". The silks had been stolen in Edinburgh by Brodie and his accomplice – the pair are believed to have been the inspiration for Robert Louis Stevenson's Dr Jekyll and Mr Hyde.

By the nineteenth century Froggatts Yard, itself, was able to contribute a number of fascinating tales of criminal activity. Happenings at one small beerhouse in the 1860s give an insight.

The Travellers Rest was kept by Frederick Andrews. In 1868, Andrews was charged with violently assaulting his wife, Selina. Andrews had asked Selina for details of his expenditure. Selina provided the information but, for her trouble, was punched so hard that she suffered severe injuries to the "lower part of her body".

Frederick Andrews, in his defence, argued that he was usually a good husband but had hit his wife because she had insisted on following him as he went out. Andrews was sentenced to six months imprisonment with hard labour.

Andrews' absence did little to raise standards of behaviour in that part of Froggatts Yard. A few weeks later the Travellers Rest was to become the focus of investigations into the death of Mary Ann Biggin.

The report of the squalid circumstances of Mary's final days was carried by the *Derbyshire Times*. Froggatts Yard is described as a "very low place" and the Travellers Rest was the lowest in a yard like that".

Mary Ann Biggin had once been the respectable wife of a grocer – Joseph Biggins. Sadly, following his death, she had fallen upon hard times and had taken up with some undesirable company.

Mary Ann found herself sharing a single room in the Travellers Rest with Frank "Ginger" Brown and four other people. Her situation was deemed to be shocking and revolting. the *Derbyshire Times* condemned "a state of things in a civilised country which was horrible to contemplate …that in a great town like this there should be people living together in a state of concubinage and sleeping in the same room."

Two weeks before Mary's death she was in Froggatts Yard in the company of "Ginger" Brown. He gave her a severe beating and she was "bleeding profusely". At the inquest, Selina Andrews, herself a victim of

Low Pavement – the desperate poverty of the Yards was shielded by this frontage.

domestic violence, was asked to give evidence.

Selina was reluctant to answer questions and only did so in "an unseemly manner". She confirmed that she had seen Mary in bed and, clearly, suffering from her beating. Selina recalled that Mary's " eyes and nose were very black". Mary had declined the offer of a doctor and, according to Selina, "seemed right enough".

The police found it difficult to find any witnesses willing to speak up or attend. At the eventual trial of "Ginger" Brown much hinged on the evidence of two surgeons.

Mr Bluett discounted Brown's view that Mary Ann's excessive drinking had been the cause of the damage to her brain and the real cause of her death. Mr Robinson disagreed and asked the jury to give "Ginger" Brown the "benefit of the doubt".

The jury came down on the side of Bluett. Frank "Ginger" Brown was found guilty but only sentenced to five years penal servitude. As Brown was led away he paused to to fix Mr Bluett with an icy stare and said "I wish you had to stop with me, sir !"

Frederick Andrews' beerhouse in Froggatts Yard continued to foster violent behaviour. In 1873, Andrews, now released and reconciled with Selina, was, himself, assaulted by James Lee. The latter was fined ten shillings for his trouble.

The degenerate lifestyle of Mary Ann Biggin would not have raised many eyebrows in Froggatts Yard. In the same year as her unfortunate death, two prostitutes were given the "default" ten shillings fine of the time. Martha Bennett and Elizabeth Epperson were both aged just twenty – the latter also known by the alias "Darkey Liz". The pair were drunk and engaged in a fight of some quality at eight-thirty on a Monday evening.

Catherine Holland also found herself ten shillings lighter. She was drunk and incapable in Froggatts Yard in the early hours of Sunday morning. Catherine was found by P.C. Else lying in the gutter with an old skirt tied around her head. P.C. Else picked her up and took her to the lock-up. He provided Catherine with coffee and some bread and butter. Any gratitude Catherine may have felt did not extend to breakfast – which she threw at P.C. Else.

Froggatts Yard was not a place to stray into unawares. Two pork butchers from Sheffield had ventured into the narrow street in 1864. They were promptly set upon by two locals – Patrick Dooley and Simon Ward.

Dooley offered to fight one of the men. His intended victim was baffled and declined the invitation. Dooley continued anyway and grabbed the man by the throat before wrestling him to the ground. Dooley, then, and with considerable practiced dexterity, rummaged in his victim's trouser pockets.

The other innocent gentleman was then punched in the mouth by Ward. The two assailants then ran off but were soon apprehended. One month hard labour each was the outcome.

Drunkenness, violence and robbery were commonplace in Froggatts Yard for much of the nineteenth century. Poverty, also, remained a feature of life there. In 1888, Martin Riley, a labourer living in Froggatts Yard , was found guilty of begging in Holywell Street. His possessions give an insight into the times. When searched he was faound to have ten pence in his pockets, seven pence in one boot and one shilling in the other. He also had some potatoes and a spare pair of old boots. Perhaps, by this time, the Magistrates were tiring of seeing residents of Froggatts Yard. Riley was given a caution and discharged.

The whole "Yards" area occupied a wide swathe of Victorian Chesterfield. Falcon Yard, Theatre Yard, Browns Yard and

The Yards today.

The Peacock Inn – Froggatts Yard was to the rear.

Castle Yard all had tales to tell. However, an area to rival the depravity and desperation of Froggatts Yard was that known as the "Dog Kennels". These dwellings were to be found at the southern end of what is now Tontine Road. The heartland of the Dog Kennels was situated between the old Slipper Baths and the historic bowling green.

Life in the Dog Kennels was in keeping with the name. In 1874, Patrick Fog was charged with assaulting Ann Gilmore in the Kennels. Fog had chased his wife into Gilmore's house. He took a knife to her before she refused to give him sixpence. Ann Gilmore bravely intervened. Fog knocked Ann to the ground and kicked her in the head. Fog denied any wrongdoing but his protestation of innocence was ignored. Fog, like many others, was fined…ten shillings.

Tragedy was never far away from depravity. In 1867 an inquest was held concerning the death of Henry Crofts, aged four months. His mother, Jane Crofts, was a prostitute who lived in the Dog Kennels.

Jane maintained that Henry had died of convulsions. She had had six children – two were stillborn and the other four had all died of convulsions at a similar age to Henry. Mr Bluett, the surgeon later to fall foul of "Ginger" Brown, was of the strong opinion that Henry Crofts had either died because of neglect or as the result of the administration of some narcotic substance. Indeed, Bluett had attended Henry a few days prior to his death. He had instructed Jane Crofts to go to the "Union" – she had refused.

A colourful resident of the Dog Kennels was Annie Basely. Annie was referred to in the local press as the "Comical Article". Comical she may have been – but she was responsible for her own mini crime wave.

In 1887, the "Comical Article" was charged with being a common prostitute and behaving in a riotous manner in the "Dog Kennels. P.C. Wray had heard a commotion in the early hours of the morning. He discovered Annie screaming, breaking windows and disturbing the whole neighbourhood. She made a long, rambling statement saying that a gentleman with whom she had been living had assaulted her. The "Comical Article" was sentenced to fourteen days hard labour at Derby Gaol.

The "Comical Article" may have told some truth. In a matter of days, Vincent Silcock of Newbold was arrested for assaulting Thomas Johnson. Johnson had been hit because he had tried to defend Silcock's first victim – Annie Baseley! Silcock received …a ten shilling fine.

Legal proceedings appeared to have little effect on Annie. In 1888, the "Comical Article" pleaded guilty to being drunk and disorderly on Newbold Road – not far from where Vincent Silcock lived. The "Comical Article" received the ten shilling fine.

The Dog Kennels are only commemorated by the antics of its Victorian residents. Their location,at least, can still be traced as you make your way into what remains of the Yards.

CHAPTER TWENTY-FIVE

Sebastopol, Stonegravels to Spital

Spital Cemetery, for many years, was the site of an unmarked grave that had a direct link with an entry in Queen Victoria's personal journal. A local campaign led by Margaret Pratt in 1969 was instrumental in the grave having an appropriate headstone. Today it commemorates the final resting place of Sergeant William Coffey V.C. D.C.M.

In 1855, William Coffey, a young Irishman, was serving in the British Army. He found himself in the midst of a key event in the Crimean War. On 29 March a live Russian shell fell into a British trench outside Sebastopol. William acted instinctively and bravely. He ran to pick up the live shell and carefully threw it back over the parapet – seconds before it exploded. In doing so, he saved dozens of colleagues as well as himself.

William Coffey's bravery was recognised by the award of the Distinguished Conduct Medal. He also received the French "Medaille Militaire" from Emperor Napoleon III for "valeur et discipline".

Back in London there was a feeling that acts of bravery in the Crimean War ought to be recognised by an exclusive award. It was decided to introduce the Victoria Cross – fashioned from metal from captured Russian artillery. The very first investiture was planned for June 1857 and records were carefully scrutinised to identify the initial, elite band of recipients. William Coffey was one of only two N.C.O.s included.

Queen Victoria was introduced to William, and he clearly made an impression. She made a note in her journal that he was "a gallant and promising young soldier".

William Coffey continued to serve and was promoted to the rank of Sergeant. He moved on to India after the Crimean War came to an end. There he was caught up in the events of The Indian Mutiny and received another medal.

William remained in India and experimented with civilian life before

The church at Stonegravels.

signing on again. He stayed in the sub-continent until 1868 when he was deemed unfit for service and pensioned. His final discharge papers describe him as a "labourer" – that being his occupation when he first joined up in County Limerick. The papers also tell us that he was aged 37 7/12 years, 5ft 8 ¼ tall, with a fresh complexion, hazel eyes, dark brown hair and, amazingly, no marks or scars!

William Coffey and his new wife made their way back to England. They were helped to settle by Sergeant Patrick Gainey – an old colleague of William's as well as his new father-in-law.

The Gaineys had found work at Stonegravels in Chesterfield. In April 1875 William Coffey moved in to "Park View".

Stonegravels, in 1875, was far from being a healthy place to settle. The year before, Dr Thorne had produced a damning report on the area. Stonegravels had grown rapidly since the sinking of new coal mines. Newbold-cum-Dunston, of which Stonegravels was part, had increased its population considerably by the time of the census in 1861, but by 1871 it stood at 4590 – a further increase of fully 30%.

In September 1870 the new status of Stonegravels was marked by the consecration of its own church. The Lord Bishop of Lichfield attended the first service in a building "well lighted on all sides" and with "windows glazed with cathedral tinted glass". The church was "warmed by hot water". Its plumbing was far superior to that installed in more modest dwellings

Stonegravels, despite its rapid growth, did not possess the sanitary requirements of an urban district. There was no system of sewage disposal. The drains that did exist were linked to open ditches, water courses, old mine workings and cesspools. There were numerous examples of larger cesspools being created which caused flooding to streets and cellars as they filled and overflowed.

Stonegravels was noted for a "great neglect" of its streets which were mainly unpaved and uncared for. Overcrowding meant that cottages were built too close together and "privies" lay within four yards of the dwellings.

One report on the conditions in the house of Patrick Quinn was typical – "there were eight persons sleeping in one room – him, his wife and three children in one bed. In another bed there were another three children. The amount of cubic feet per person was calculated at 85 instead of the required 300."

The main street from Chesterfield through Stonegravels had raw sewage slowly seeping out of a raised bank on which roadside houses stood. In the school at Stonegravels, more than one hundred children were sent home on the same day because they were all suffering from "rigours and vomiting".

A great many colliers lodged in the area – even though there were no registered lodging houses. Scarlet fever was endemic and deaths from "diarrhoea and fever" were commonplace. A report by Dr Macintosh found that sewer gas found its way into houses because sink pipes and drains were poorly constructed. At the Prospect Inn the cellars were full of contaminated water. The urinals emptied directly into an uncovered ashpit.

Sadly, William Coffey quickly fell foul of these living conditions. A matter of months after settling in Stonegravels he was dead. He died of "chronic diarrhoea" in the presence of his wife on 13 July 1875.

The circumstances of his death were, for a while, disputed. There was a story that he committed suicide in a barracks in Sheffield but this is almost certainly a case of confused facts and mistaken identity. The Chesterfield death certificate is quite clear and specific.

William Coffey, and his fate, are the subject of a folk song written by Graham Cooper which was performed by "The Lonesome Travellers". The first verse poignantly mentions his "plain" grave in Chesterfield.

The Victoria Cross won by William Coffey is now proudly on display at the Kings Own Borderers Museum in Carlisle.

The one remaining town centre memorial to William Coffey V.C.

CHAPTER TWENTY-SIX
Transportation, Elopement and Paupersim

In 1871 a well-regarded local Police Superintendent was approaching retirement. Superintendent Raynor reflected upon some key cases in a long career fighting crime in Derbyshire and the North Midlands. An incident in Brackenfield many years previously was recalled in some detail.

Raynor, as a young officer, had been assaulted in Nottingham by a villain by the name of Davis. The latter had been sentenced to ten years transportation.

In 1849, fate was to bring the two men together again when Raynor chanced upon Davis in a public house. Davis was rather uncomfortable at being recognised but, then, went to great lengths to reassure Raynor that he had changed his ways since his return.

However, shortly after the chance encounter, Davis and three accomplices returned to criminal ways. The gang broke into the house of John Newton, an elderly bachelor who lived in the quiet backwater of Brackenfield near Ashover.

There was a belief locally that there must be a tidy sum of money kept on the premises. This was based on the fact that Newton had always been prosperous but seemed to spend little.

The four masked intruders, once inside Newton's house, made their way quickly upstairs. They guessed that was the likely hiding place for any of Newton's savings.

John Newton, although advanced in years, was still fit and strong. He met the gang at the top of the stairs – armed with a scythe.

Davis, not a man to shirk a challenge, was the first to approach. Newton told Davis to stop or face the consequences. Davis responded with a stream of abusive language.

Newton decided that Davis was not the kind of man to be reasoned with and promptly struck him hard on the top the head with the scythe. A circular piece of flesh and part of an ear were sliced off the unfortunate Davis.

The other members of the gang made a chaotic and rapid retreat down the stairs. Somehow the detached flesh found its way on to the top of a milk puncheon where it was retrieved and slapped back on Davis' head.

Steadfast, Newton remained at the top of the stairs throughout. The burglars disappeared into the night.

Next morning, as news of events in Brackenfield spread, Sharman, the keeper of the lock-up in Alfreton offered some thoughts. He was convinced that a gang of man from Nottingham had committed the break-in.

Acting upon Sharman's hunch, Raynor was able to renew his professional acquaintance with Davis. Raynor barged his way into Davis' home and, undeterred by the screaming Mrs Davis, apprended the heavily bandaged criminal before the latter could his hands on a long dagger kept by the side of the bed. A search of the bedroom revealed a pistol in a coat pocket and the black masks worn by the Brackenfield burglars.

Raynor, and colleagues who assisted in the arrest, were awarded £5 each by the Court. Davis received another ten years transportation.

A decade later, John Newton was to endure another attempt to rob him in his home. A travelling tinker called upon Newton to sell him a shirt for a shilling. Newton, rashly, agreed and in the process of payment revealed a bulging purse. The tinker snatched the purse and made good his escape.

Foolishly, the tinker decided to return after dark. He quietly broke in to Newton's kitchen and helped himself to a snack. His movements awoke Newton. Comically, the tinker made various noises in an attempt to convince Newton that there was a large gang present.

The intruder, clearly unaware of previous events in this Brackenfield house, made his way upstairs. He encountered Newton armed not with a scythe but with a hatchet. The passage of time had not diminished Newton's resolve …or his aim.

The tinker was floored with a single blow. He was carried away to the Alfreton lock-up where the man needed the urgent attentions of the local surgeon. Local Magistrates all gave Newton a sovereign each in recognition of his outstanding bravery.

Elopement in the nineteenth century was associated more with shame than romance. It was a term that described a wide range of extra-marital activity often reported in graphic detail in the press.

In April 1880, the *Derbyshire Times and Chesterfield Herald* commented that the area was gaining an uneviable reputation for "elopements". The newspaper then went on to report on the romantic entanglements of an anonymous Chesterfield vendor of "a certain succulent".

The gentleman in question was a married man who had fallen for his neighbour's wife. The reporter found this rather surprising as the lady was, apparently, regarded as "not particularly attractive".

Notwithstanding, the lady in question found herself waiting at Chesterfield Railway Station at five o'clock one Wednesday evening. She was expecting to be joined by her amorous neighbour. The pair were planning to travel to Sheffield together. The lady waited alone for over an hour before deciding to board the train at twenty minutes past six. Whilst waiting she had taken the opportunity to send a telegram to the missing gentleman.

The telegram was delivered, but after the intended recipient had already left for the station. It was read instead by the man's wife.

The aggrieved lady made great haste to Chesterfield Station, accompanied by her son. On arrival the pair secreted themselves and observed the errant husband board the next train for Sheffield. They then, quickly, boarded themselves – taking care to occupy an adjoining compartment.

The end of the journey on Sheffield Station platform was not a happy one. The husband was confronted by his furious wife and son. The situation worsened as the neighbour's wife appeared. Only the arrival of the Police prevented a violent outcome.

The aggrieved wife and her son returned to Chesterfield, leaving the "lovers" behind. The newspaper, still diligently on the case, reported that the pair were still in Sheffield.

The law often played a part in Victorian elopements. In March 1883, a Brampton husband invoked a clause of the recently amended Married Woman's Property Act. Henry Austin was a publican and shopkeeper whose wife had "eloped" with his brother, William. Mrs Austin had taken her ony child, a girl aged eleven, and some money.

The Married Woman's Property Act helped women in that they had control over their finances. Henry Austin argued that, because finances were now separate, his wife could be charged with stealing some of his money.

William Austin and Mrs Austin were found in Liverpool where they had been living as man and wife since their elopement. Mrs Austin was arrested and brought back to Chesterfield. William Austin was allowed to go free as it could not be proved that he had appropriated any of his

Midland Railway Station, Chesterfield.

brother's property ...just his wife!

"The Derbyshire Times" was pleased to report that an agreement had been concluded between the parties and no further action would be taken.

Pauperism was another term common in Victorian life. Chesterfield, like many industrial towns, was able to provide many examples of how society dealt victims of poverty.

William Brown was charged with being a "dirty pauper" in Chesterfield in 1863. The Governor of the Chesterfield Workhouse, Mr J.H. Ramsden, said that Brown had wilfully dirtied his bed clothes and the floor of his sleeping quarters. Brown pleaded guilty and received a sentence of fourteen days imprisonment – not entirely appropriate for a man apparently incapable of keeping a cell clean.

A few years later, Ramsden had occasion to bring a "disorderly pauper" to Court. Ann Flaherty had refused to do chores in the Workhouse and, moreover, been abusive to Mr Ramsden. Fortunately for Flaherty, Ramsden was not present in Court to give his evidence. She escaped with a caution – with the rider that any repetition would result in twenty one days hard labour.

Charlotte Alford was not so fortunate. She was charged with being "drunk and disorderly whilst a pauper". She had enjoyed a day's leave of absence from the Workhouse rather too much. She had returned "intoxicated" and asked to be discharged. When her request was refused she had proceeded to smash up the washroom windows – causing ten shillings worth of damage. Sadly, her previous poor record went against her and she was sentenced to one month hard labour.

In 1879, there was an unusual case of a pauper campaigning for his dignity. A man called Higginbottom, aged seventy-five, argued that being forced to pick oakum was not a suitable activity for a man of his years. The Board of Guardians of the Chesterfield Workhouse treated his argument with some respect. They believed that the man's heavy drinking prevented his family looking after him outside the facility but that picking oakum was within his capability. They resolved to leave the final decision with the doctor.

This, slightly, more balanced treatment of paupers was echoed by the fact that girls in the Workhouse in 1879 were "fairly well taught". In the same year, the pauper children also received a rare treat as Mr Marsden, manager of the boats on Mr Irving's dam at Walton, invited them to have a ride.

CHAPTER TWENTY-SEVEN

A Burning Effigy, Violence and Shameful Behaviour – the Life and Work of a Victorian Vicar

Crich is a pleasant village in rural Derbyshire. In the last quarter of the nineteenth century the spiritual well-being of this diverse community was the responsibility of Reverend William Acraman. Rarely has a local cleric attracted so much attention.

In 1883, Crich was in the midst of a heated debate over the local headmaster. Mr Scott had been a popular and very successful incumbent. He had presided over significant growth and development at his school in Crich. However, Scott had lost the favour and support of Reverend Acraman as disputes fermented as the result of tensions with Baptist villagers.

Acraman was a strong character. He was a prominent figure in the temperance campaigns of the time. His zeal had attracted the attention of Florence Nightingale whose family lived locally.

Florence Nightingale was very concerned about the general behaviour and moral standards in Crich and its neighbouring hamlets. She was particularly worried about antics in the Wheatsheaf Inn. Nightingale took tangible steps to wean the locals off their dependence on alchohol by opening a tea shop.

Florence Nightingale took the time to write to Reverend Acraman praising the work that he was doing within his community. She enclosed three guineas to help with his campaign and concluded – "I trust that your fight in favour of temperance will be crowned with success. I pray to God to bless your work."

Acraman and Nightingale were facing a genuine challenge. A few years previously drunkenness had triggered a very dramatic incident in Crich.

P.C. Mee, the local constable, had arrested William Cowlishaw for being drunk in Crich. The usual practice was to escort the prisoner to the nearest

Reverend Acraman of Crich.

"lock-up" in nearby Belper. Unfortunately a crowd of between forty or fifty Crich gentlemen decided to stalk P.C. Mee and his charge.

From a safe distance, Andrew Blackwall offered Cowlishaw his advice – "Farmer (Cowlishaw) don't go with the bastard any futher...come back!" P.C. Garrett, who was accompanying P.C. Mee, told Blackwall to desist and go home or he would be arrested himself.

Blackwall did, indeed go home. He quickly filled a ginger beer bottle with gunpowder and fashioned a fuse out of string and cloth. Blackwall then proceeded to attempt to bomb the Crich Police Station !

Fortunately, the "bomb" failed. P.C. Mee returned home to find the shattered remains of the bottle and gunpowder spattered up ten feet of the building. The serious incident was made worse by the fact that P.C. Mee's wife and children were inside the building during the attack.

Blackwall was found guilty after a search of his property revealed a stock of similar bottles – all made by W.E. Burrows of Derby. A local weaver identified the cloth wrapped around the bottle as being from the same material as some belonging to Blackwall. The judge, summing up, described Blackwall's actions as "cruel and unmanly". He sentenced the Crich bomber to seven years penal servitude.

In February 1883, a meeting held in the village to discuss the controversial case of Mr Scott the headmaster, was potentially equally combustible. Scott had now been dismissed and many present blamed Reverend Acraman for the decision.

Debate was heated and a scuffle broke out as Acraman and his curate, the Reverend Blair, attempted to leave. At first the curate bravely placed

The church in Crich.

himself between Acraman and a group of angry villagers. The curate found himself "roughly handled" as Reverend Acraman was bundled through the door.

A few days later Elijah Kirk, a local draper, and Samuel Bennett, a frame-work knitter, found themselves facing a summons for assault. The vicar said that Kirk and put his fist up to his face in a very menacing manner. Bennett, he claimed, had propelled him out of the meeting room. Acraman also accused Bennett of encouraging the boys of the village to "shout and hoot" at the two Crich clergymen.

The vicar requested police protection. He maintained that he would have suffered injury had he not been a rather tall strong individual. Reverend Blair had not escaped totally unscathed although his injuries were only described as "slight".

The alliance between Acraman and Blair would prove short-lived. A matter of weeks after the ill-tempered meeting in Crich's Independent

Clubroom the two clergymen were wrestling each other on the floor of the Vicarage!

In March 1883, Reverend Acraman had written to the Bishop of Lichfield complaining about Reverend Blair's conduct. Unfortunately for Acraman, his curate had been forwarded a copy.

Blair was determined to read aloud the contents of the critical letter at a parish meeting attended by Acraman, Mr Hunt J.P., Dr Dunn and the secretary Mr Saxton. The appearance of the letter prompted an instant reaction from its author. Acraman launched himself towards his aggrieved curate and made a grab for the document.

Blair's reflexes were up to the task and he was able to keep hold of the letter. Acraman then grabbed Blair by the collar and pulled him to the floor – smashing a dining room chair in the process.

Hunt was forced to intervene and managed to pull Acraman off the captive curate. The latter was then helped to his feet by Dr Dunn.

Hunt, a local resident of considerable standing from Alderwasley Hall, suggested that the parish meeting probably ought to be concluded. He told the bemused Mr Saxton "not to enter the last episode in the minute book." Hunt, correctly, took the view that the versions of both protagonists would soon be aired in court.

Indeed, in April 1883 a hearing at the Belper Police Court found Reverend Acraman guilty of a "technical assault". He was ordered to pay a small fine and pay costs.

Acraman's guilt was welcomed and celebrated in Crich. Later that evening a gang of men made their way to the Market Place. They had with them a pole with a large effigy of their vicar attached.

A crowd soon gathered and there was a brief discussion about the next step. It was decided to erect the effigy in a field facing the Vicarage. The effigy was then set alight. The head fell off as the flames took hold, it was then kicked around with considerable enthusiasm.

Events took an even more sinister turn when an individual in the crowd began to conduct a mock funeral service over the embers of the effigy. The words were greeted with loud cheers.

As the fire died down, the mob moved closer to the Vicarage and shouted abuse for more than an hour.

The controversial Reverend Acraman continued to find it difficult to keep a low profile. In 1885 he was arrested on another charge of assault. On this occasion his alleged victim was James Wright, an eight-year-old boy. There was little evidence and the charge was dropped.

In 1899, though, a case was brought against Reverend Acraman that would astonish even his staunchest critics. The Vicar of Crich found himself on trial for a number of offences relating to his inappropriate behaviour towards Ada Flint – a Crich parishioner aged just thirteen.

The scandalous tale shocked the local community. It emerged that, at one point, Acraman had offered to marry the girl.

Reverend Acraman was found guilty of committing indecency with Ada Flint. The judge, in his summing up, made the observation that for a man of Acraman's background to behave in such a fashion was "a hundred times worse than ignorant men". The judge went on to say that he believed that it was his duty to sentence Acraman as severely as the law of the time permitted – imprisonment and hard labour for two years.

The sentence caused gasps in the courtroom. Acraman was visibly shaken but recovered sufficiently to make a plea in mitigation.

The Reverend said that he had been misled as to Ada Flint's real age. He thought that she was two years *older* that she actually was. He produced a copy of the baptismal register to corroborate his claim. He said this proved that she was now sixteen and had left Crich Carr School "a long time since" – she was of an age to " begin work in the mill".

Moreover, Acraman claimed that *he* was actually *older* than people believed. He explained that his health had been affected by the strain of the case and prison would be hard for him.

The judge rejected Acraman's plea for some mitigation. The prison doctor, he said, would take care of Reverend Acraman's health.

CHAPTER TWENTY-EIGHT

A Footnote in Calow –
Edward's Coronation
Brings Little Change

In the summer of 1902 The White Hart at Calow was at the centre of a notorious murder. Most murderers go to extraordinary lengths to conceal their crime – not so John Bedford.

Bedford called into his local as usual for some beer and a chat with his associates. He was on his second drink when the conversation, unusually, turned to the prospect of "swopping trousers". Bedford mysteriously proclaimed that his trousers would "be neither good to me or thee before long".

The assembled company was intrigued by Bedford's remark and began to press him for an explanation. Bedford took a fellow drinker, Fred Wagstaffe, to one side and stunned him with the revelation that he had killed Mrs Price – a lady with whom Benson had a long-standing adulterous relationship.

Wagstaffe was, initially, dis-missive and responded in typical Derbyshire fashion – " Get on with thee, soft !"

Bedford, though, was deter-mined to move swiftly towards the gallows. He held up his leg and presented his blood-stained trousers and boot for Wagstaffe's inspection. The latter was now starting to be a little more convinced.

Bedford was either eager to unburden his conscience or had his

The White Hart, Calow.

Royal Patronage in Chesterfield in 1902.

judgement affected by the ale he had consumed. He produced the key to the Price's cottage and told Wagstaffe that he would take him, there and then, to view the body.

Fred Wagstaffe was rather wary of bumping in to Mr Price in such circumstances but Bedford put his mind at rest, saying that the unfortunate and unsuspecting spouse was in Chesterfield staying with his brother-in-law.

Just in case there remained any shred of doubt about his guilt, Bedford addressed the drinkers in the White Hart. He announced that he had killed Mrs Price and "locked her up for the night". At this point he theatrically produced the key to the cottage again as tangible evidence of his control of the situation. His drinking companions responded with laughter and cries of "shut up!"

Wagstaffe, though, decided that he would accompany Bedford down the winding lane to the home of Mrs Price.

On the way they chanced upon Robert Davidson who was persuaded by Wagstaffe to join them. Although Benson, known locally as "Tommy", had the reputation of being "a quiet and peaceable fellow" – Wagstaffe was beginning to feel rather edgy.

The three men arrived at the Prices' cottage. It was of a quaint traditional design and half hidden by foliage. The garden in front of the small windows was well-stocked and well-kept.

The scene that greeted them in the cottage was not so picturesque.

The body of Mrs Price was lying on the couch, the front of her head smashed in and covered with blood. Indeed, there were blood stains everywhere – the ceiling and walls were liberally spattered.

Bizarrely, there was a stocking on her left hand and a darning needle in her right. Evidently, Mrs Price had been taken completely by surprise. The murder weapon, a short poker, was stained with dry blood.

Bedford surveyed the scene and left the cottage with Wagstaffe and Davidson. He paused to lock the door but only after finally addressing the tragic figure of Mrs Price with the words "Goodbye, darling, I have loved thee, but thou has deceived me."

Wagstaffe was immediately helpful in his advice and said "Tommy, give me the key. Thou will have to go with me. I will take thee to a Doctor."

Davidson, though, recognised that Bedford was not looking for excuses for his behaviour, saying – "He doesn't want any insane petition getting up. I know he wants to die for her. I should not offer to get him off."

Therefore, the murderer and his two friends returned to the White Hart. A postman who was passing was called across and asked to find a constable.

P.C. Outram arrived in the Tap Room and mistakenly arrested Bedford for the murder of "his wife" – an error of detail Bedford was quick to rectify. Bedford the looked around him and, in a reference to the recent accession of King Edward, proclaimed "This beats all your Coronation!" He then burst into song with a rendition of "Goodbye, Dolly, I must leave you!" as he was led out of the public house.

The motive behind the murder was simple – jealousy. The forty-one-year-old Bedford had taken up with the forty-eight-year-old Mrs Price and visited her frequently over a number of years. Her husband was not a man of good health. Mr Price had suffered serious injury whilst working at Hartington Colliery but, if this wasn't bad enough, he had been knocked down, at a later date, on the Great Central Railway.

Consequently, Mrs Price had assumed the role of bread-winner. She was described as "of good build, homely appearance, scrupulously clean and hardworking." She sold fried fish from a small shop near Arkwright Town Bridge.

Recently, the relationship between Bedford and Mrs Price had been compromised by the rumoured appearance of another – younger – gentleman as a rival for the lady's affections. The identity, or, indeed, existence, of this person was never confirmed.

Mrs Price had been drinking "hop bitters" with "Tommie" Bedford in the White Hart at Calow shortly before her murder. They did not appear to be drunk and seemed on good terms.

Mr Harrison, the landlord of the White Hart was surprised at the subsequent actions of Bedford saying "He was the last person that anyone would expect to do such a deed. He never seemed to have enough stomach for anything of that kind."

However, some White Hart regulars recalled the jealous Bedford declaring, on more than one occasion, that he would kill Mrs Price.

Bedford was sentenced to death. He met with his family in the days prior to his execution and expressed his remorse for his crime.

When daylight broke on 25 July 1902 Bedford awoke from a reasonable sleep and felt able to eat a small breakfast. He was then taken out to meet his executioners – Billington and Pierpoint.

Billington was short, stocky and muscular and described as a "bulldog individual of the seaman type". His father was a famous executioner.

Pierpoint was taller than Billington. His family was also involved in this grim occupation.

Bedford looked unkempt. His moustache had grown into an untidy beard. His resolve to accept his fate evaporated on his way to the scaffold as he broke down and wept. His handkerchief, which he had been holding to his tearful eyes, was taken from him. His cap and scarf removed. His shirt collar was unfastened in readiness for the noose.

The public had little sympathy for Bedford. His execution failed to cause any great interest and the usual hoisting of the black flag outside the gaol did not take place. The small gathering outside simply had to take their cues from the comings and goings of officials who needed to be present and the tolling of the bell.

Shortly after 8 a.m. the sound of the bell signified that Billington and Pierpoint had efficiently calculated a drop of seven feet and the sentence had been carried out.